Celestial Promise

Hayley Ann Solomon

Proverse Hong Kong

2017

Celestial Promise is the winner of the International Proverse Prize 2016 Supplementary Prize.

In this collection of poetry, written over half a lifetime, Hayley Ann Solomon focuses primarily on the pursuit of excellence, immortality achieved through finite life, love in all its forms, and social justice. As it waxes and wanes, the collection cycles through sequences of lyrical ballads, sonnets, elegies, haiku, snippets of nonsensical verse; all blended with a substantial dose of existential philosophy and social comment.

The collection covers a full spectrum, from the darkest psycho-social moments, to zeniths of absolute joy. The liberal use of consonance, assonance, alliteration, echoes and half-echoes, rhyme and cross-rhyme make for a style rich in sound-play. This, together with strong metrical awareness – very often iambic or trochaic pentameter and tetrameter – evokes a flow that is quite typically euphonic. There is therefore a sense of lyricism despite a broad diversity of topics and moods.

The anthology evolves to become a promise of regeneration, in synchrony with the phases of the moon, from which it takes its celestial title.

CELESTIAL PROMISE

Hayley Ann Solomon

Proverse Hong Kong

Celestial Promise
by Hayley Ann Solomon
1st edition published in paperback in Hong Kong
by Proverse Hong Kong, under sole and exclusive licence,
November 2017.
ISBN: 978-988-8228-73-7
Copyright © Hayley Ann Solomon, 2017.

Distribution and other enquiries to:
Proverse Hong Kong, P.O. Box 259, Tung Chung Post Office,
Tung Chung, Lantau Island, NT, Hong Kong SAR, China.
Email: proverse@netvigator.com;
Web: www.proversepublishing.com

Available from https://www.createspace.com/6790322

The right of Hayley Ann Solomon to be identified as the author
of this work has been asserted by her
in accordance with the Copyright, Designs and Patents Act 1988.

Cover design: Raoul Solomon

All rights reserved.
No part of this publication may be reproduced, stored in a retrieval system, or transmitted, in any form or by any means, electronic, mechanical, photocopying, recording or otherwise, without the prior written permission of the publisher. The book is sold subject to the condition that it shall not, by way of trade or otherwise, be lent, re-sold, hired out or otherwise circulated without the publisher's prior written consent in any form of binding or cover other than that in which it is published and without a similar condition including this condition being imposed on the subsequent owner or purchaser. Please contact Proverse Hong Kong in writing, to request any and all permissions (including but not restricted to republishing, inclusion in anthologies, translation, reading, performance and use as set pieces in examinations and festivals).

British Library Cataloguing in Publication Data.
A catalogue record for this book is available
from the British Library.

Introduction

Ah, the moon.

Her phases are as predictable as the tides she governs, as transient as the light she casts. Her transitions have inspired this work; moments of extreme brightness and shattering submissions to dark.

This anthology waxes and wanes, from the lyrical to the classical, from the ironic to the heroic.

The collection cycles in many forms from hope, wisdom, joy, philosophy to despair, cruelty, the nonsensical, and ultimately, like the phases of the moon itself, regeneration.

Phase I: Waxing
Philosophy and inspiration

Phase II: Full Moon Brightness
Laughter, romance and a sprinkling of bright nonsense

Phase III: Waning
Deeper contemplation and darker motivations

Phase IV: New Moon Darkness
Grief resolution, social conscience, regeneration to light.

Life has a cyclical structure, but is never absolute. So, too, the topics reflected in this collection.

It is an inspiration to me that in exploring the astronomical phases of the moon, I find there is no finite 'dark side', only an inevitable movement of the lunar hemisphere towards light. This is the celestial promise, and the promise of this collection.

I hope that the reader will smile, feel and dream with me through all the phases, remembering that the light of the moon, whether faded or far, is always, always extant.

Hayley Ann Solomon

Table of Contents

Introduction	5
Contents	7

Phase I: Waxing — 11
Philosophy and Inspiration

Freedom won	13
Do not sip from the cauldron of common	14
I'm bound by the weave	15
Once grown, now gone and green no more	17
I am not alone	19
Intimations of him	22
If I could capture a glimmer of happiness	24
It was always a gift	26
Bands of the spirit	28
Tangle, tangle your fingers in mine	29
The blink	32
Chess	34
Sonnet	37
If I could clutch a far off dream	38

Phase II: Full Moon Brightness — 41
Laughter, Romance and a Sprinkling of Bright Nonsense

For this one night	43
Said the thorn to the scented rose	45
A thousand snowdrops and a rose	47
To jump on a bunk	49
Quirky cooking	51
Up on the farm at Marybank Rd	53
On challenging a speed fine	56

Upon receipt of three sons	58
A beauty I could never be	60
Divine comedy	61
Mr Mathematical	62
Financial wizardry	64
The reading quest	66
A nymph to the goddess	69
A pot for my pit	71
I will live with thee and be thy love	75
My son if you please, drops his 's's, drops his 'gs'	76
Bliss bedazed (or ABC)	78

Phase III: Waning 81
Deeper Contemplation and Darker Motivations

The mirror	83
Quartet of haiku	86
Give me the time of day	87
Opal Fields	89
Like a jute sack	91
This vast valley of sound	92
Paradise	94
I'd rather bear a fractured heart	97
Cogito ergo sum: ode on intimations of dementia	99
Freedom lost: a contemplation of child labour	101
You, who are my friends	103
Not for me the niceties	105
My whispered wish	107
My air will be your aria	108
Dell of dreams	110
Dare	112
To die for	114

Phase IV: New Moon Darkness — 117
Grief resolution, Social Conscience and Regeneration to Light

I'll watch how wild the poppies grow	119
Annette	121
Give not, grant not	123
In Memoriam: September the eleventh	125
When shall we five meet again?	127
Elizabethan sonnet 1: Compare me not to some sweet summer's day	129
Elizabethan sonnet 2: My master's eyes are nothing like the snow	130
Mantra of the living dead	131
Greek mythology cycle: Songs of the Siren	134
1. Ballad of Strimadees	134
2. Betrayal of Persephone	137
3. The sirens to the mariner	141
4. Circe to the sirens	143
5. Regeneration	145
Fear: a palindrome	147
Joy: a palindrome	148
I am the moon	149
Epilogue	151
Advance response: Randal A. Burd, Jr.	153
Advance response: Viki Holmes	154
About the Author	155
Notes	157

Phase I
Waxing

Philosophy and inspiration

Freedom won

When daylight dies and darkness knells,
with sinking sun in sea-soaked swells,
when petals pout in shaded dells
and demons dance in mind-made hells,
Oh then I beg,
oh then I plead,
do not the silent shadows feed,
nor lust upon the salted mead,
despair's last cup,
dank-dry with need.

Do not pleasure them
that see your pain,
let solace small
that still remains,
echo in its hushed refrain,
echo slow
and soft restrain
the breaching of your heart's domain.
Linger long on bright beliefs
that shelter shade from darker griefs.

For, in gazing not 'pon spite's
death-night,
but holding fast to candle light,
to dawn, to all small sources still,
but bright,
a thousand wrongs may yet become
a thousand rights in song and sum;
a million fragments once begun,
of truth,
commitment,
freedom won.

Do not sip from the cauldron of common

Do not sip from the cauldron of common:
its flavour is kind,
but tastes not of content.
Find yourselves wellsprings of fresh wet, wet, wildness
– drink with the dawn,
not yesterday's scents.

Do not sing silently my little lions,
but roar your vast visions,
vie with the middling,
master the mean.
Waiver life's average –
its medium's mentor.
Roar, as you rip at ordinary's dreams.

Then,
you may build
where boredom once bled,
laugh at obstacle's head,
confound all conundrums
in logic's lithe tread.

Build yourselves castles, my little lions –
surpassing
the probable,
peaking
the perfects.
Then,
in threads of impossible,
build
towers erect.

I'm bound by the weave

I live in a space
that is half mine and half place:
mind-twine,
that unravels like yarn on the floor:
half my hopes, half my fears,
and yet, there's still half more.

Impossible to grasp, though I yearn and I clasp,
and am sometimes almost content
but there's always that twine, that flex that is mine;
and it clings to my thoughts like contempt.

Unreachable rope, such unteachable hope,
so silken, so smooth in my hands:
if I only could reel
the thoughts that I feel
in the sweetest of tidiest bands.

But no!
My yarn is a-mess, a mass of mind-stress,
it twists in some hopeless looped ties.
If I could weave I might spin
the mess that I'm in
or brighten my thought with wool dyes.

But I'm tangled for sure in the dreams that allure
and in fears I find hard to define,
so I'm bound by the weave,
seem set to deceive,
I'm all snagged and enmeshed and wool-shot,
I'm twisted, I'm turning, bewildered I'm yearning,
I'm bound by some knotted mind-plot.

Unbind me oh please, in satin soft breeze,
untwist and untwirl me a lot;
cotton untie, unflex by and by
keep whirling
my mind- muddled-knots.

Now
my thoughts are a ream
of ribbons unseen,
you turn them to silk with your smile.
The twine, though it's mine, you soft underline,
in petal-soft swathes in a pile.
You lift up a strand as you stretch out your hand,
my yarn runs ribbons so free.
Alas you're a rogue, but your kiss is in vogue;
And my thoughts?
They're as silken as me.

Once grown, now gone, and green no more...

Lest the earth grow warm beneath my feet
and summer solstice turn to heat,
lest rhythms of the greenhouse sun
bear down on me,
the sated one –
sated with a life replete,
dappled by swift pleasures' mete,
too quick to care, the air replete with factory fumes and
fossils' sleet,
lest the earth grow warm and cooling ice
like ribboned rivers
carve and dice
our planet earth not once, but thrice,
from north to south the polar ice,
and searing rains on forest floor –
the stumps of trees,
once grown,
now gone,
and green no more.

Oh, yes:
It's water's rage and waves of ice
that drown,
then drain,
in eon's trice.

Lest no one listen,
I will, wind,
I'll sing your song and caution bring.

Come beckon
fire, earth and air,
I'll touch with care
your free fruits fair.

Celestial Promise

And, plucking fruits,
I will allay
the wild of winds and plant, I say,
the seeds for hope
for morrow day –
from sapling tall to caraway.

I will not take without true need.
nor need so much I turn to greed.
The earth's small hints are mine to read,
so heed I will –
I will indeed.

I am not alone

On the banks of the Rangitikei,
I dabble my feet.
It occurs to me that though I am wet,
wet-washed with sand,
salted by wind, and silent,
I am not alone.

Far,
high in the headwaters,
high,
high in the Kaimanawa,
the waters rush wet and wild.
The river stirs with its first intimations of
joy,
and begins its long,
life-giving journey,
its odyssey of twists and turns,
plateaus and cliffs,
birdsong and silence,
to reach me,
and my cold, sun-dappled toes.

I am not alone, though my thoughts are bleak.
Behind me, Vinegar Hill,
breathtaking
and breathing with life.
Before me the kingfisher and tui,
then all the little stick insects
that drink and drift on branches.

The little creatures, the shy and the busy,
crawling, chirruping,
in a day impervious to us and our bustling humanity.

And the characters.
Not just here, but everywhere,
everywhere I care to look.

I once made the acquaintance of a kea.
He looked me in the eye, cocked his head and I could
swear I saw him wink.
Then, with a busy swirl of green, he took off, teasing.
I searched for him again and again,
and though I heard him,
as I tiredly trudged
half-way up the McKinnon pass,
I saw
neither him nor my lunch.

Not so the Weka.
He I glimpsed many a time,
shyly extending his neck here and there,
scurrying across my path, busy, busy,
looking for the next shrub or shelter.
Once he stopped, eying my pink shoelaces with
fascinated absorption.
I think he forgot to be busy, then,
for he hopped on my boot and began the serious
business of exploration.
I have never, I think, felt so honoured,
or remained quite so still.

Then again, on Doubtful Sound, with the engines off
and not a whispered voice or human step
to quell the rustling of the wind,
the insistent song of the bell birds,
the whoosh whoosh of Kereru,
the tiny chirrups of fantails,
the distant calls of shags and gulls and gannets,
squawk-chattering, squeak-chirruping,

water water everywhere,
from gentle rain to the dripping of epiphytes,
more normal than our roads and our rules,
our laws and our constant press of civilization.

I stand with my sister and gaze at the stars,
luminous with familiarity though we live eons apart,
half a world away, separated by oceans,
but not hemispheres.
Matariki – Pleiades, the Southern Cross,
glittering constellations that twinkle in shifting skies,
her night, my day, my day, her night,
but always there,
always a constant to be invoked,
no matter how far our separation.

Not so the birds.
These are so vastly different that the sounds are
incalculably irreplicable.

I startle as a feather touches my feet.
It is so perfectly formed, it is almost precious.
I pick it up and put it in my pocket.
It has been marked by millennia.

And I?
I breathe, my thoughts thirsty for content.
I shed my weariness
as the subtleties of birdsong absorb me,
absolving me of a day
of the witticism and worries,
so solely,
so wholly
the strange domain of men.

Intimations of him

May the raging of oceans
call forth your name
as thundering cumulus
foreshadows your face.

May ancient wild winds
insane and insane,
rip at the roots
and the wild thorns
again, yes again.

Take sand-soaked seas
and lush lilacs blowing,
take crushed camphor colours
and bend us, allowing
torment's sweet fingers
its silence, its scents,
the quivering quiet in
the whispered,
the meant.

Bend us and bind us,
bond us so much
that shivering-soft sands
shift restless to touch
and are warmed and are warmed
with impossible heat,
as senses awake,
as melt-mind-mingled we meet.

And all around, in echoes, in trees,
in woodlands and forests,
in lightening,
in breeze
the world is awaking,
alive and alive,
for the grasses are singing,
brooks bubbling,
banks brimming,

wet wild birds
are bringing
on wing and on whim,
intonations of poignance,
of passion,
of power,
intonations of perfect,
intimations of him.

If I could capture a glimmer of happiness

If I could capture a glimmer of happiness
and twine it on my tongue,
I'd taste it there forever,
and thread it through my song.
I would sing both high and low,
so soft and aching-sweet,
I'd trill the arc of rainbows,
I'd thrum each slow heart beat.

If happiness was a thread,
and love its silken strand,
I'd wind it through my fingers
and palm it in my hand.
It would feel, I think,
gossamer soft,
or gleam with inner light;
but happiness is no single strand
to be captured on first sight.

No, I guess it is a cloth of life
woven from all threads;
the aching and the pure,
the browns as much as reds.

It's a recognition,
sometimes hard to see,
that every peak has shadow,
as every branch a tree.

If one can look upon one's life,
and see that cloth all sewn,
here and there with holes,
here and there wind-blown,

If it meshes, all, to keep me warm,
and loved ones feel its lace,
I guess
it's then the closest cloth
to love's light-soft embrace.

If I had such a cloth,
and it slipped a tiny seam,
if a single strand escaped it,
then perhaps I'd have my dream.

It was always a gift

You worried so much that love was a trap,
you hardly believed your heart.
I, stubborn, refused to relieve you –
and stoic – refused to part.

Love is never a silken web that softly ties and winds,
if ever a person finds it so, rip, rip and break the binds.
Love weaves not to capture,
nor to stop one in one's tracks:
It cocoons one in a shimm'ring cord –
onwards,
never back.

The cord it is of silver,
so soft a moonbeam sleeps,
it stretches ever further, it cherishes the deep.
And the deep is in your eyes,
the deep is in your heart,
it weaves the aching longing,
but never binds with art.

Rather, it ribbons up our souls,
it stitches yours and mine,
by a starlight stream of lightness
is the stretching, silk-soft twine.

"So," you may think,
"A silken trap – soft, but still a vice!"
"No", I say, "listen well,
and look, not once,
but oft-times twice."

For though love is gentle,
fragile its portrayal,
the ribbon will snap
like shattered glass at tiniest betrayal.

The splinters can shatter your soul.

And mine?
Mine they can pierce,
for the ribbons of love run red
and the wrench of a parting's fierce.

But our ribbons,
they linger on,
soft as a star-lit stream,
light as a single strand of silk,
this long,
long beribboned dream.

Far they will remain so,
forever, yes they must,
for passion's forged our friendship,
and time has burgeoned trust.

The love you once feared was never a trap
as only time has proven.
It was always a gift,
a silken thread,
once wound,
once bound,
once woven.

Bands of the spirit

Unknotted from time's
tethering tangle
a single-strand moment rises,
ever rises, like a phoenix from flames.
Unleash a wisp of smoke curling
from warm-whistling burning,
burn brightly burning,
mind mirror the yearning.

Capture the second,
that sweet, soundless second,
when forever fills fully
the dreams that we seek.
Rise like a phoenix,
oh mystical moment,
and bond us,
as always,
in bands of the spirit.

Bind us for always,
for far
and forever,
cloak us,
oh moment
in time's tangle-soft raiment.
Cloak us
completely –
For love's perfect
we keep.

Tangle, tangle your fingers in mine

Like the branches of some brazen tree
tangle, tangle your fingers in mine.
I, twine-like, will do the same
as we cross this bridge boldly.

Below us,
the river will race with dizziness
and the sky, so high,
will lull this day
with a soporific sweetness.

I look at neither.
Only at you.
You are my world.
My zenith and my deep desire,
my fire and my light.
You,
keeper of my hope and
half- wish.
Their buds of intent
wait only for the blossoming.

Come, seeker,
we will cross this bridge together.
We will amble along its surface
as one, and feel its weight.

We will touch the cracks with our toes
as the river rages beneath us,
a tantalising dance
of sun-slipped splash,
dapple-dark wells and
swells, swells of running water.

Celestial Promise

We will walk
as the sun taps through the wood of our bridge.
We will find,
find each forgotten nail hole,
each knot in the timber of time.
And the sky – the very sky – will warm our backs.

We will not hurry across this bridge,
but talk as we amble slowly.

When it sways,
we will throw caution to the winds,
and thrill to the danger.

When it is still,
abandoned by the breezes,
creaking with
ennui,
we shall yet not
weary of the walk.

For each step
is the echo of
your breath on my hair,
and each tread
the steady beat of your heart.

These are what matter.
They are nearer than the water
that ripples across the stones,
nearer than the reflection of that
lazy, azure sky.

We will cross the bridge smiling,
and when tears,
unbidden,
streak our faces,
we will take comfort in the tangle of our fingers
and not loosen our hold.

When the sky darkens with rain
and the river below us
slows to bleakness,
we will not stop walking.
We will feel the rain on our faces
And embrace even the wet.

Blossom,
buds of the half-wish.
Blossom,
Your time will come.
We will wander across this noble walkway
With friendship's fingers
that never,
never let go.

The blink

I blink
and soak
in the secrets of your gaze.
I have known you forever,
'though it is but a moment since our meeting.
How fleeting is that bold transition,
the one from stranger to friend!

How endless the truth
that wends its way from mind to waiting mind.

Mine is the thread of fine filament
that weaves, in a single whisper,
the pattern of your simplest thoughts.

Yours is the satin,
that slow, soft, ribbon of rest
that stitches our soul.

There is no "ought" in this,
or "why?" or "what?" or "should?"
there is no "but" in this,
but a blink.

I drift on that blink,
winking not at the sky
but the sun,
the sun,
whose orbit is mine,
and at you,
the pivotal one.
I am not inured to your shadow,
nor unfazed
by the setting of sky.

If I ask "Why?"
my tongue
evades me,
but the blink –
it's that blink
that has taught us
to fly.

Chess

There's a war in our world and it mirrors our mind.
There are seekers and finders, assassins with skill,
sentries as binders – with queens who will kill.
Oh, there is dancing at court, the slow exposition,
of pieces with power – and state acquisition.

In a hall of bright mirrors or out on the plains,
gambits are offered, peace waxes, peace wanes.
Envoys all smile, but they know their own fate –
death soft approaches – as silent they wait.

Yes, in silence and stillness, forward pawns creep,
bold and defending, soft spoken and meek.
The first to suffer in this war of the wise,
expendable tools in the name of surprise.

Ah… then enter the battle, those sleek, brazen spies,
bishops of power, strategic in lies.
And let no one think,
oh no knight or fine king,
that their stealth was not meant,
or their blades without sting.
For, sending page 'pon some mission,
to threaten far knight,
they reveal their true selves
with the stealth that's their right.
By making no move, they've gained line position –
strategic advantage – the spy and his mission.

And as for those knights, with their thund'ring power –
they puzzle the lines, awaiting and dour.
'Pon war-horses braided, they leap fortress and walls,
to capture the squares thought safe from all squalls.
They defer to so few, but the rook is their master.

Celestial Promise

Yet, Castle's a fortress, averting disaster.
He cares less for battles, for banner's first dead. –
He cares for his king, defends majesty's dread.
So he'll castle, all pensive, that masterful rook,
his actions defensive as he rests in his nook.
Rests, but not sleeps –
for when battle-field's cleared,
when deaths on both sides
have been counted and teared,
he will waken and win – both attack and defend –
the might of the rook is then without end.

And what of the court, the king and the queen?
What of the reason this carnage that's been?

Well, the queen is a warrior,
she might start the war late,
but no piece is e'er safe from her shattering gait.
She stalks across field, she marches through mire,
no piece is more perfect, no power more dire.
But wait! The queen must have grace,
she must stop first and think,
for enemy will slay,
will unthinkingly sink any life for that life,
any noble at all, to cause death to the queen –
cause majesty's fall.

And what of the king?
Oh, he's laggardly passed, a poor kind of leader who
leads from the last.
He hides, if he's wise, in a fortress of stone;
he moves not at all, lest he's caught on his own.
Oh, the kings are quite feeble, but when pressed to die,
a king and poor pawn can give death the bold lie.

As for pawns,
let no-one call those foot soldiers weak,
for if first forgotten in their soft-steps so meek,
if first they are scorned, then slow and unseen,
the lowliest of pawns might become a crowned queen.

There's a war in our world and it mirrors our mind.
If chess is the game, the answer's sublime –
oh, for every tiny battle lost,
see the faults,
count the cost
but don't resign –
don't think it ever –
The noble heart will e'er endeavor.
The greater plot is often won,
as battles lost
are wars begun.

Sonnet

How shall I define content? Not by tongue,
for tongues are speechless in the face of bliss.
Nor yet by heart or hope or lung,
the trio oft ascribed to this.
And why not heart? For hearts might bleed.
And why not hope? For hopes are dreams.
And why not lung? For lungs but breathe.

Content's not brilliance – it shines and gleams,
with softer truths and heartfelt dreams.
Its hues are subtler cast, those soothing beams
a-glow, a-drift, beribboned reams
of star-touched sands in shadowed creams.
Caressed by kindness, love's intent,
the sweetest kiss marks deep content.

If I could clutch a far off dream

If I could clutch a far off dream
and hold it by some silk-soft seam,
I'd feel its warmth and inner glow,
I'd hold it still – then let it go.

For what are dreams
but wistful's wish?
Or hope's sweet gift
in sleep-filled kiss?
Oh,
if ever dreams they had a name
I'd say it clear
that you once came.

But you are not some silk-soft trance,
nor shadow's light
to tease and dance;
nor figment fine
to still enhance
the window
of my wounded soul.

You, my dear,
my trust enchants,
your warmest truth
my waking grants.
No dream or fancy,
just perchance
the kindest keeper
of my living whole.

Oh dearest one!
so close you are,
so warm to feel,
captured in my heart's ideal.
A dream, perhaps,
but one that's mine.
A dream,
but with its place in time.
One for me to ever hold,
Enraptured by my heart,
ten-fold.

Phase II
Full Moon Brightness

Laughter, Romance
and a Sprinkling of Bright Nonsense

For this one night

For this one night,
I am yours, and you?
You are mine –
mine to woo and want.

Slip softly into silence
as you wash away the world.
Seal your lips with open heart
as mine, already waiting,
are stilled with quiet wonder.

Take my key,
and unlock time.
Silence-slipped,
it waits,
as I do.

Let our eyes embrace,
and in that gaze of gladness,
find our friendship full.

Let us need not words –
there are none bright enough,
light enough,
for this moment of
melt-mind-meeting.

Kiss me with your eyes
and I will kiss with mine,
for this one night,
and future's more,
let us linger a moment
on the shores of sweetness,
storing our words,

in hearts, in minds
in the soft slowness of sweet discovery.

Let the air not breathe,
nor the moon's glow shine,
'till you whisper my name
and I,
dare-dreaming,
answer thine.

We shall speak,
when we have found.

Said the thorn to the scented rose

Said the rose to the thorn,
"I wish you weren't born;
You prick and I despise you."

Said the thorn to the rose,
"As everyone knows,
I protect and don't revile you.
What would you be, without prickly me?
The answer might stun and surprise you!"

Said the rose to the thorn,
"I'd not be forlorn;
I'd bask in my petal pink glory."

Said the thorn to the rose,
"That only just shows
you only see half of the story."

"Oh," said the rose, in her prettiest pose,
"What tale can there possibly be?
I scent and I swell;
my blossoms pray tell,
are passing pleasing to see."

"Well," said the thorn,
"You'd wish you weren't born
when your nectar's all dried up and sucked;
when you're plucked from your stem,
and cut once again; without charm
and with even less luck."

"What charm?" said the rose,
"I can only suppose
that you think you might keep me from harm?"
"With my charm", said the thorn,
"I will keep you on form,
for prickles deter and alarm.

"If insects approach,
or rough hands try and poach
your silken, oh petal soft bud,
I'll cut and I'll pierce –
I'll slice something fierce –
And all in the name of my love."

"Oh," said the bloom (with a blush deep maroon)
"I hadn't realised your talent.
I wish I'd not said I quite wish you dead,
for your kindness is really quite gallant."

So the thorn and the rose,
they willingly chose
to love one another at whim.
The thorn with a hush, the rose with a blush
buds the brightest of blossoms –
for him.

A thousand snowdrops and a rose

Float softly through my consciousness
like a bubble in a breeze,
fair and light
and simple-sweet,
whole and calm,
a quaver-beat of radiance a-glowing.

I watch you in my inner dreams
a bubble, ever growing,
slower than a passions' whim –
but feather-light and knowing.

Knowing, sweet,
that passion's whim
may soon be swiftly spent,
but bubble's joy is unalloyed
by darker sentiment.

Ever-light, it floats on love,
enwrapped in petal-scent,
a thousand snowdrops and a rose
is dawn's kind testament.

The snowdrops are its clear white sheen,
the rose its blushing glow,
and in its circle love's agleam
in iridescent flow.

Drift across my consciousness
that I might live my dreams,
brush across my waking hours
in radiant hues unseen.

Unseen by all who burst through life,
whose bubbles are ill spent,
but seen by me, oh purest one,
who loves with heart unspent.

Let me feel, with fingers light,
the circle-surface, where,
with trembling awe and utmost care,
I'll reach my dream-joy fair.

Touch my love and drift in flight,
my bubble-sweet temptress,
a thousand snowdrops and a rose,
in bubble-light caress.

Drift across my consciousness
with trust your truest kiss
enfold me in your snowdrop trance
as we dance, we touching dance,
the meaning of this bliss.

To jump on a bunk

"Raphael, Raphael, Raphael," say I,
"What are you doing, bouncing so high?
With your hands on your head,
Feet-foot-flipping – ahead,
You'll do a wrong-wriggle and fall off your bed!"

"Oh, never, oh never, oh never,"
cries he,
"I'm as high as a giant, as tall as two trees.
I'll bounce on this bed for as long as I please,
For if I fall on my fingers,
I'll land on my knees!"

Then he bounced with a giggle,
A gurgle of glee,
Like Tigger he bounced, so springy you see!

"Use the ladder," I cry, "It is there for good purpose,
Climb down from the top,
From that sheet-shambling surface.
Yes, I know you can jump,
But you surely must not."

Bump, bump, bumpity bump,
The mattress on top gets a hip-hopping jump.
I open my mouth, I open it well,
My tongue and my teeth
Get ready to yell.

Then a question arises,
That halts my attention,
A curious query that I really must mention,
"Raphael, is that fun?"

He grins and he nods."It's as fun as can be,
this bunk has got spunk, it's as spunky as me!"

I swallow my yell and climb, by and by,
to the top of that bunk, to my son up on high.

He helps me right up, with a squirm and a wiggle –
To kiss – but not cuddle – my mad-muddle-middle.

I bounce in that bunk,
We bounce there us two,
for if Raphi's a tigger,
then mum must be Kanga,
And baby Rhaz,
'Roo!

Quirky cooking

This is the preface to a full recipe book I've written in rhyme – one of my more ambitious and decidedly quirkier projects!

In the cupboard of dead utensils,
I keep my grander plates –
the ones that need hand-washing,
and consequently hate.

In that same cupboard,
deep in inner gloom,
Lie half a dozen lids –
and a long forgotten broom.

The lids have no tubs
and the tubs have no lids,
I am perfectly certain
none ever did.

Nothing fits – there's half a beater,
dented cans – a dust defeater.

Stuffed in there, find you can,
every gizmo known to man.
Most need cords and have them not,
I've searched and searched –
then looked a lot.

Nothing can be thrown away
lest cord is found another day.

I must confess, I'm no mechanic –
the kitchen stuff just makes me panic.

So, empty handed, all forlorn,
a quirky-cooking chef is born.

To bear this title, have this pride,
no utensils must abide.
Shut the cupboard, shut the door!
This is what this rhyme is for!

Caveat...
I will relent a smidgeon – not too much –
and allow a little bit of stuff:
A microwave
(essential for this credential);
Slow cooker
(doesn't have to be a looker).

I grudge a beater
– but hey, ok –
but pots and pans must go away.
Ok! Ok!
One of each may sit and stay,
but if black or burned, just throw away.

No graters, no blenders, no grinders, confess,
I hate them all, could not care less,
they glug up my cupboards, they just make a mess.

They really should vanish, should never be seen –
they waste all my time, just needing my clean.

So,
Quick and fast, that's my test;
quirky cooking at its best!

Up on the farm at Marybank Rd

Up on the farm at Marybank Rd,
Ralitza is barking at Rascal the toad.
Rat-a-tat rooster is pecking at worms,
while Rhapsody hen
is clucking in turns
at Radish the cow and Rat-a-tat
who,
besides being a rooster,
has nothing to do!

But Radish the cow is earning her keep,
grazing the grass with Rambo the sheep.
As for Rocky and Reason, the two little pigs,
they're pruning the vines,
they're rootling for figs!

Three pairs of boots come hurrying past,
Raoul in the lead, Rhaz at the last.
Muddy those boots, and wet, wet with dew,
but gambling-great-gummies,
good gummies and new.
Over the gates they clamber and climb,
Raphael in front, Rhaz far behind.
For Raoul's in the middle,
one can tell you can see,
for his head is the tallest,
the tallest of three.

Mince for the turtles and Gobble gets seed.
The ducks and the peacocks, the geese and indeed
every fair friend,
whether feathered or not,
gets something to eat from
Raoul's bucket-like pot!

Celestial Promise

Rat-a-tat rooster is 'waiting his grain
as Rhapsody hen's
pluck-pluck-pecking again.
Ralitza stops barking as three boys appear,
but Tusha and Truschka now take up the rear.
With Minka they yap, so loud and so long,
it's a symphony of sound,
four Samoyed-dogs strong.
As for Ralitza ...
Round the paddocks she runs with a rush,
past Rambo the sheep,
past dad with her brush.
Will she ever be groomed,
that puppy princess?
Her papers are perfect,
but oh what a mess!

How muddy her paws,
how tangled her locks,
'cos she buries her bones
and chews on old socks.
Now, with a satisfied wag,
she returns to her bowl;
she eyes her big bones,
swallows half of them whole!
The remainder are buried,
with doleful delight,
in the soily dark hole
she digs half the night.

Silence and peace, but no! It is not!
For Gizmo is staring – she's staring a lot.
So silent and still, one can so scarcely see,
that Gizmo is staring,
safe-snug up a tree.

Celestial Promise

Gizmo the cat, who thinks it's not fair
that Ralitza the princess
is stealing her share.
Not food of course –
she scorns those old bones –
but the boys and the brush and her Marybank home.

Ralitza the friendly, Ralitza the brave,
dances in circles, barks at the knave.
And all the while stilly,
safe up the tree,
Gizmo just sits, oh, so silkily.
Perhaps here a growl, perhaps here a purr,
but Gizmo the cat's immaculate fur
moves not an inch,
oh no it does not,
as she stares at Ralitza,
stares at her a lot!

Then out of this mayhem comes Tush with a rush.
Ralitza is quiet,
come Rhaz, Raoul and Raph.
Gizmo has vanished,
but where can she be?
Not hiding above, not high in that tree!
But creeping right back,
through green Gizmo-grass,
Creeping right back, to her place in the house.
For Ralitza the princess,
for all her proud line,
must stay right outside,
come rain or come shine.
So all is at peace, at Marybank Rd
and the night is so still –
'cept that turkey and toad.

On challenging a speed fine

John, we take delight in your quest to seek what's right.
By dawning day and darkest night,
we've come to watch for flashing lights.
Not because we travel fast
(though naturally we're never last!)

But
because we've come to know
that tiny towns are always slow.

Tired of watching gardens grow,
the cops are keen and on the go.
They ticket in the wind and snow,
they stop the morning traffic flow.
They set up road blocks any time;
they only want to fine and fine.
Their egos seem to be anointed
the more we get demerit pointed.

Sad, so sad, it's way unfair.
We feel your pain – we've travelled there!

In one week,
my dear beloved and a clicking camera
– undiscovered –
met perchance on daily basis! –
I'm still not back to homeostasis!

Now, fight, oh John,
in the name of all,
answer, please, the pressing call.
Remember, do, the need for truth,
and most of all, question proof!

Calibration information
is the vanguard of our nation.
By what means and distillation
have we met these obligations?
Check this out
with vim and vigour –
We count on your aplomb and rigour.
You speak for us, and all those caught,
who speed by chance,
not blatant sport.

Upon receipt of three sons:
Gentle advice to babysitters

They're not good tidy-uppers,
our merry little men,
but a gentle nudge here and there
should stop you falling down the stair,
over toys, under dens,
caught by snippings, caught by pens.

And when it comes to suppers,
that trio of tidy-uppers,
might chorus you with wills and won'ts
with wails of "yum!" and willful don'ts!

But rather than please too freely –
(for what can one do really?)
When two like nuts – the other not;
when three like grapes – but not those "dots",
when one likes stew – but then there's two –
Oh, what does one do?
Offer in lieu?

No! One surely does not!
Three boys and only one pot.
An everyday rule –
yes, we're nobody's fool,
porridge for dinner more often than not.

It's all quite hopelessly humdrum,
this everyday conundrum,
For rice is "not nice" –
but fruit is a breeze,
you can fill them all up
on some bread and some cheese.

No curries, no spices,
nor anything "nices"
(for one who loves hot food like me),
but blatantly bland, like jam, understand,
should keep this trio of three.

It's easy, as easy can be,
this clear-cut recipe. –
If they're naughty, it's stock.
If they're good, the Great Wok
and in-between plums from the tree.

Most important of all are the cuddles,
the quintessential huggles.
Don't stint, dare I say,
lest they clear fade away
to a trio of snuggle-less puddles.

Now we'll stop our connivin' and plottin',
for our wisdom will soon be forgotten.
I just bet that we'll say, after two nights away,
that our trio's been spoilt
wholesomely rotten!

"Nices" is a made-up nonsense word to add humour.

A beauty I could never be
Ode to my manicurist – with a laugh and a giggle

A beauty I could never be
without Miss Lang to oversee
each lash, each curve,
each painted nail,
such tender care,
such kind travail.
What work it is to try create
a beauty from a girl who's late.
To attempt a solemn eye-lash darkening
from a silly girl who can't find parking.
(And if I do, Miss raids the till
to fill my meter on St. Hill!)

Thirst I never shall endure,
while sitting for a manicure.
There always is,
as prompt can be,
a cup of coffee,
pledge of tea.
Then,
as late,
I wait
for nails to dry,
Miss Lang she chats
and ably tries
extracting keys
from
my mad bag,
so paint,
still wet,
won't smudge or snag.
And if it does (Oh, silly me!) she'll paint again, once
more, for free.

Divine comedy

The devil once said to an angel,
"I will manifest myself
in symbols and signs,
in vines, in serpents,
in half-light lunulate,
and the crescents
will strangle your light,
in a deeper darkness
luminate."

And the angel said,
"I thank you
for your flattery,
but your vile
and verbal battery
frightens me
not a wit.

"You have me in stitches
with your snakes
and your witches.
As for crescents
and curves,
they're
but physics in swerves.

"So...
With the caveat that you're dark,
there's nothing I shall hark,
for I freely admit,
I find you a twit,
and your threats,
quite simply,
a lark."

Mr Mathematical:
a jargon rhyme quite graphical

Mr Mathematical
is really quite fanatical.
He lives on pi and chi,
and many meals quadratical.

The angle of his sleeping
is really more in keeping
with theorems
that he's seeking
on his master-maths sabbatical!

It's a truth that when he slumbers,
his head is full of numbers.
His dreams are filled with reams
of quotients,
mids
and means.

By day it's really "stagerous", the keen use of
Pythagoras.
And his clever use of power
multiplies each second hour.

"There is nothing," he says,
"like squaring hard work,
unless perhaps it's to try
to *cube* it perhaps
and unless there's a lapse,
success must surely apply."

Mr Mathematical
never shirks the work or
slacks on stats.

He might seem extreme
– a pox on lax! –
but his numbers glean
the meanest stacks
of quantum leaps in whites and blacks.

"Life is not linear,
it's certainly graphic –
it's eqi and quadri and long,
before I could count, my mind was a fount –
but my thinking was quaint and quite wrong.

It's numbers, you see, that make up a me,
and thinking is clearer and free
when two precedes three and four is no more
the square root of six than folk lore."

So while he's on sabbatical, his mind adrift emphatical,
he winks and takes off hattical, to future minds
"theor'attical"!

"Stagerous": a made-up nonsense word derived from "staggering", to add humour.
"hattical" and "theor'attical" are also made-up nonsense words, to add humour, the latter derived from "theoretical".

Financial wizardry

A frown furrows my beleaguered brow
as piles of paper – I don't know how,
strewn and scattered across my room,
reminders all of sometime soon,
sometime soon when I'll revile my studious lack of punch and file.

Sometime soon when I'll begin my frenzied search of rubbish tin.
Not just bin, but shelves and drawers,
I've disobeyed all finance laws,
I've let the contracts pile and fall
behind the cracks against my wall.
I have no idea where they've gone,
those monthly statements, one by one.

As for premiums, or what to pay –
I'll save that for another day!
I need not panic, feel bereft, save searching for those docs I've left,
the ones I know I was meant to file – they're stacking up
by yard and mile!

But wait, anon, I'll not despair, before I tug at roots on hair,
'ere I sink in dreary gloom, or face the foulest paper doom,
I'll phone my friend at MAS,
the one with flair and fine address,
the one whose "no's" become a "yes" –
From life, to health,
to income stress.

I'll phone her up and then I'll see
the lengths to which she'll go for me!
Patiently, and with a pen, she marks for me again,
again,
oh yet again, the dues and dates, the when, oh when.

Oh sublime relief!
I hold the sheaf in my hand,
of all I need of growth and land,
of 'surance figs and income stats,
I have it all – the whys and whats.

I have it all, so now I'll reap
those piles of paper in a heap!
Fearless, now, I'll empty bin
my stuffed full, graceless, rubbish tin.

Free at last
I'll throw and cast
the papers all from first to last,
all except that one clear letter –
Sandra, dear –
it could not be better.

"MAS": Medical Assurance Society

The reading quest

Well, boys and girls, take a look –
Zappo fell inside a book.
No-one could be more surprised
than Zappo –
who was mesmerised!

At first the writing made no sense, boldly black and
dark and dense,
but as he stared, he felt much better –
each curvy angle made a letter!
Each letter linked to make a word,
each word a sentence, I have heard.

Now Zappo knows it's rude to stare,
but some strange magic happened there.
The words all rhymed, when strung along,
to form a zippy Zappo song.
And the song went ...

Zappo, Zappo can't you see,
you're inside a dictionary?
All the words there'll ever be,
belong in here the inventory!
So if you're quick and take a peek,
my page will turn to what you seek.

But who is that? What's the matter?
It's Alice, dears, and old Mad Hatter.
Turn the pages, turn them do –
there's Thing One and there's Thing Two!
No, turn some more, I want to meet
Cinderella down that street.
Tane Mahuta and Hawaiki,
Hine or Maui, oh come ... quickly.

Zappo Zappo don't go far
that is where the wild things are!
Jump to pages seven and nine
to duel with kings in olden time.
Grab a helmet, take a sword,
Merlin waits and you're a lord.
Lord Zappo?
Now that's real funny,
but not so strange as Pooh bear's honey!
Sweet and sticky, gold and runny,
it can't fill up a small bear's tummy.

Zappo, Zappo can't you see
You're inside a dictionary?
All the words there'll ever be
belong in here the inventory.
But if you're quick and take a peek,
my page will turn to what you seek.

Mrs Dis-com-bob-ulous
Margaret Mahy's one of us.
Wave hello to Toad and Otter, fly a broom to Harry Potter.
Tired of wizards? Take a turn,
there're crazy things for you to learn.
And learning makes us grow and feel;
learning makes our world more real.

Maths in puzzlers to keep our minds busy,
tongue twisting testers to make our teeth dizzy.
Hey! There's the girl who sells seashells on the seashore,
turn the page quickly in case we find more!
Peter Piper's picking a peck of pickled peppers –
Hurry, hurry, we don't like pepper –
turn the page to something better!

Celestial Promise

Back again to true, true tales
of Southern Cross and northern gales,
how to bungy, how to draw,
Zappo reads about them all.
Then,
mind the dragon on one-one-two,
he's breathing fire
– he's close to you!

Zappo, Zappo can't you see,
you're inside a dictionary?
All the words there'll ever be
belong in here the inventory.
But if you're quick and take a peek,
my page will turn to what you seek.

Lowly worm, and Where's that Wally?
The Water Hole is down that alley.
Do I hear the jungle drums?
Boom, bom, boom, bom,
Zappo feels it loud and strong.

Sometimes stories are sad or frightening,
Christchurch quakes, or lost mums, lightning ...
But keep reading reader, don't you cease –
after storms there's often peace.
And every word has its place,
every letter linked and laced,
every story you will find,
stretches Zappo's magic mind.
Come imagine,
come and read –
reading quests are quests indeed.

A nymph to the goddess

I offer myself to the goddess of beauty
and hope that she answers my call,
I would rather be pretty inside and out
than richer than Croesus at all.

Oh, Aphrodite,
I will offer my plea, in hopes
that I win your heart,
I'm plain and I'm poor,
I'm mortal for sure,
but my dreams still set me apart.

And whilst speaking of beauty,
(your private domain)
I ask that you help me to sing,
such sweetness I've heard in the cadence of word,
there's beauty in all that you bring.

Now, you are my muse and I chose you well
for, whilst beauty is what you bestow,
the love that you guard
as a god that is hard
is more than I ever could owe.

If I sing like an angel,
both mellow and high;
If I fit the fine clothes
I never can buy;
If I find my true love
(and he's a god of a guy!);
Then I'll believe;
I shall ne'er deny
the domain of my goddess,
oh beauty on high.

Celestial Promise

So, dearest Venus,
your starrier name,
I ask that you blink and you pause,
bind me with beauty
and find me my love,
for I always espouse your cause.

And if you don't,
or can't,
or plain, plain won't,
I'll still sing your praises, I vow,
I'm bigger than sulking
or scowling
or skulking
I'm pretty inside, right, right now.

So, no bargains from me,
I'll straight set you free,
a mortal can't purchase devotion.
But,
if you don't mind,
and if you are kind,
perhaps –
the tiniest potion?

A pot for my pit

One day when my room
is mad-mess and mad-muddle,
I climb on my dad
for a kid's kind-a-cuddle.
He whispers a story,
he hums me a rhyme,
He tickles my toes and I laugh all the time.
I laugh and I laugh till my tummy feels funny,
a rumbly-tumbly-nose-runny-funny.

He says to me,
"Hey, you should not be inside,
You should build in your sandpit,
You should slide on your slide.
You should play with your digger,
your boat and your ball –
You should play with your toys.
You should play with them all!'

And I think of all this, my thinking quite bland,
as I jump on my digger and head for my sand.
I dig and I dig a very deep hole,
a hole that is dark, a hole that is whole.
I dig with my spade, but that proves too small –
so I dig with my fingers,
I dig with them all.

I love all the sand,
every last bit.
I scrunch up my toes and feel my feet fit.
All 'round my tummy and on top of the ground,
is loose sand I've been digging, loose sand that I've found.
I need a bucket – but there's none in my pit.

Small cups I've a-plenty,
but none of them fit.

What a shame, what a shame, what a pity say I,
As I think and I think how to build my sand high.
My toes in the hole,
my nose in the sky,
I think of my answer,
it comes by and by.

I need a pot from the kitchen.
I know that I do.
That pot mum bakes cakes in,
that pot to make stew!
I need that pot. I need it a lot,
a pot that's not hot,
a pot that Mum's got.

So off to the kitchen I drive in my digger
to find a nice pot,
a pot that is bigger.
Oh my, I say, oh my, my, my!
That pot is too far,
that pot is too high.
If I climb on my chair,
and tippy-toe-try,
I might touch the pot's handle,
I might try, try try try.

I wibble. I wobble.
I wig ... wig ... wig ... wiggle.
Oh, no!
Oh no! no! no!
Make that wibble unwiggle!
I am not going to go!

I am not going to fall,
not fall at all!

Kerrrrash!
I come down with a bang!
A big clitter clatter,
Then that cling and that clang.
I fall with a shriek. I fall with a yell.
Those clink-clanking cups are not whole,
I can tell!

I bump on my bottom.
I pick up a lid.
I sit on the floor.
I think what I did!
I scrunch up my face,
my mouth does a wobble.
I think and I think.
I think I'm in trouble.

Trouble it is. Trouble a lot.
I'm put in my room
to think of that pot.
My mum is not pleased,
oh no she is not.
As she picks up each piece she asks,
"Why, love?" and, "What?"
I sit on my bed.
I lick a small tear.
I sit on my bed.
It seems like a year.

What's that poking out, all shiny and red?
I climb off the pillows, peer under the bed.
If I fit a block on my crane,
then wind it all up,

find a train on the floor,
close to my truck.

Soon all else is forgot. I forget about pits, I forget about pots.
I build a tall tower,
I make a small moat.
I wonder and wonder how to make my boat float.

Then,
I jump
on my blocks!
They fall in a pile.
The door opens slowly –
I see my mum smile!
"All finished!" she says with a grin.
I hug her
and hug her 'till my daddy comes in.
He tickles my tummy, then says with a laugh
"Cute, cuddly kid, it's time for your bath!"

I'm not very pleased.
Oh no, I am not!
Well, I look at my boat,
look at it a lot!
And I think and I think ...
I think of that boat, I think to myself,
will it sink, will it float?
If I take that mug and my yacht
and my very new tug
I could have fun with the water,
wet in my tub.
Possibly.
I sigh. I ponder. Then I nod to agree.
Would you have had a bath
if you had been me?

I will live with thee and be thy love

In answer to Christopher Marlowe's sixteenth- century piece, 'A passionate Shepherd to his Love.'

I will live with thee and be thy love
and we will all the pleasures prove
that winter troubles yield not might
where every moment there shines light.

And we will sit and silent know
that what we wish shall overflow
with word, with smile, with soft, bright glow
our heartfelt sigh from long ago.
Oh,
I might pocket all your buckles gold
or pluck from posies thousand-fold.
Yet ...
no planet spinning fast and free
no continent adrift at sea
no world, no star, no comet far
can e'er be more than you to me.

For you, my dear,
encompass all,
sweeter than a madrigal,
finer than those coral clasps,
more, much more than I should ask.

And so your promise has me moved,
your tender kiss cajoled and soothed,
Your kindness 'shrined, so I shall serve
the heartsease you so strong deserve.

Devotion pure and far above,
I'll live with thee and be thy love.

My son, if you please,
drops his 's's drops his 'g's

Will I grow?
You never know!
Even on my tippy toe,
even standing row by row (brothers high and I below),
it's very sad, for I am small,
next to middle, next to tall.

I beg my brothers,
"Please go slow,
please, please brothers,
feel my woe!"

But do they listen?
Oh, no, no, no!
Their legs and arms just overflow –
Two boys high to one boy low.

I can talk quite well,
'though I think it best,
to strike from English the letter 's'.
Also, of course, there's I - N - G,
A 'diculous inconsistency.

Why say 'ing' when in's enough? –
Walkin', talkin', all that stuff.
To draw, not 'cribble -
never 'toppin',
hugglin', 'nugglin', jumpin', hoppin'.

Meddlin', muddlin', it's an art,
droppin' esses at the start.
Droppin' 'ings' is much the best,
leaves me breath to say the rest.

Celestial Promise

Chitter chatter all day long,
vocab good, syntax strong.
But when it comes to 'wim or bath,
my mum and dad just laugh and laugh.
Even when the bath is brimmin',
like all big boys ...
I love my 'wimmin'! (swimming).

Bliss bedazed (or ABC)

Anxiously angry, a bevy of adverbs beats briskly in my brain.
My capricious consciousness is beyond care.
It dares me to drop my dalliances, and for once, do
a dance of unmitigated delight.
Oh, to undam my damned defenses,
to let my eddying energies finally flow!

But fear,
fear forgets; it feasts on fallacious phantoms, fostering foolishness
in all its unfathomable depths.
I shall not be forged from burning guilt,
finely ground to the grit and grime of gloom.

"Go, ghosts!
Hear, instead, harmonies of hope."

But,
I wish I weren't still icy, seeking intrigue,
so indecisive in my inspirations.
I have such inconsistent intuition,
such intractable ideation,
that
the jaws of jeopardy kiss keen.

"Kismet!" I cry,
in a sudden calamity of self-destruction.

I loathe my lack of faith,
my listlessness,
my lingering lamentations
on love and its lack.

I've been lascivious,
lacking,
altogether lustful.

Mmmm,
maybe by moonlight
I'll make sense of my madness,
master the mischief
that makes mock of my mood.
I nod –
nine times from ten,
I need nil but a notion,
something
to numb my next omen of dread.

Perhaps I've been peevish,
too quick to quibble,
my reticence ravishing rapture.

So soothe me.

Somewhere,
a stolen joy and spilled seed
transforms sadness
to something special.

Touch me.
Transition me to acceptance.
Tell me it's true
I'm tangled in gladness.
Trust me, tell me, entwine me with love.

Under
the undulating clouds
you've brought unutterable peace.

I'm upset
it's taken so long;
undeniably,
I've been wrong.
I'm utterly,
vigorously vexed!
You've been virtue,
While I've been hexed!

Every ventricle,
every vein,
you've waxed,
I've waned.
All the time,
you've been exactly
excellent.

There,
I feel our extract of life;
that exciting, ecstatic exigency,
claiming me.

Wonder: such wonder.
Such tremulous
whisper of life in my womb.
Welcome.
Welcome, dewy youth, utmost truth.
My yin, your yang, bedazzled,
dazzling, flamed I am,
joy amazed,
zenith crazed,
phased by love:
I'm bliss bedazed.

Celestial Promise

Phase III
Waning

Deeper contemplation and Darker motivations

The mirror

A schoolgirl in a uniform,
hateful skirt with tights all torn,
Was that me, really me,
or could it be the mirror turned?
Could it be I was meant to be
the girl who ran assembly?
The girl who got to pick and choose,
those games we played – and never lose?

Never lose,
oh no, not I, the girl I was
would never cry.
She'd never ever feel the pain
of feeling lost and all to blame,
of clever (never!) coming first;
always just the plain, the plain old worst.

Was I hoping just to get a dance?
Hoping so to have a chance,
at all the things I'd never get,
fashion hems with cigarette?
Stolen kiss with sun long set,
thrilling smiles all so unmet?

"Will the mirror turn?"
I so oft yearned.
"Will the hopes of time e'er be mine?"
"Will I ever feel the sense of peace
now worn on faces liked the least?"
"Will gladness come?" I asked them all,
the mirror and that empty wall.

"Will my turn come?"
I asked again, in sentences I can't explain.

Answerless,
I'd often ask, oh, that silent looking glass.
That silent, silent, silent glass
of doubts and fears now long, long past.

For now the mirror speaks to me of love in deep
maturity.
Whole of heart,
and yes that's me –
the girl that was – soaring free.

I wish I'd known, Oh I wish, I wish I'd known.

If I had another mirror,
I'd take it to a school,
I'd tell some lonely child
to play some other rule;

to wash the glass free of fears,
to turn her back on faithless peers;
to dream her dream,
and never mind, if what she values takes some time.

For what she feels
and what she dares,
reflects her life in all its shares.

And if she cares,
oh how it's true,
her caring will reflect anew.

Let her keep the mirror.
She will find
that it is worth being alone and lost,
than losing herself.

It is worth waiting for a friend,
than forging an acquaintance.

It is worth taking pride in ones difference
than begging for acceptance.

Let the glass glimmer her whole –
inner beauty,
outer soul –
in its gleam.

Let her see
what's not been seen:
let her see
what choice can mean.

Let her feel,
feel it keen,
the present's past,
the future's dream.

I shan't forget – and never will –
the looking glass I carry still.

Quartet of haiku
(In syllables of 5, 7, 5)

1

lacy underthings
swinging in wistful sunlight,
heating secret thoughts

2

thrush singing unheard –
silk-slipping of petticoats
to moon-soaked grasses

3

glove wafts loose on breeze,
last kiss lingering 'neath moon
'till dark stills its touch

4

time broken on pegs;
winter's abandoned stockings
flap laz'ly in wind

Give me the time of day

Give me the time of day that I might take from mine
the simple solace of your thoughts
and add it to my shrine.
Share with me a single smile
and mine will dance with yours.
In my heart, if not my lips,
for you,
my sad-sweet cause.

I ask not for your hand and heart,
too wild they are, too free,
like a firefly upon a leaf
they dance – but not for me.
I watch the glow, the fluttering flames
that dance upon the dawn:
too swift to hold and never mine,
though once, once, upon a still-soft time,
I called them so.

Can I hope,
when dreams forget and tears,
wet from remembering, still soak my sheets?
Can I hope then, my siren,
that you, too, will remember?
I ask not for your hand or heart:
those, my dear, are fleeting.
I ask for more.
Yes, more than I dare
but mine,
mine by right of caring.

Spare me, Sweet,
the simplest piece of your soul;
not the restless flutter or the evening glow,
but the part that is the softest.
It is this that I crave.
Save it for me,
save it silently.

It is my abiding hope
that in the darkest of my dread dark nights,
the fleeting touch
of firefly will burn.
Let it softly burn my heart whole.

In Opal Fields

In Opal Fields he bought a jewel,
bluer than the sun-ripe sky,
yet fire flashed from deep within
and burnished greens,
like verdant grass,
gave gold
its hues.
It was a looking glass
of love
and light
and beauty.

She wears it now about her neck
and feels the blaze each waking day.
Each moment, now,
a misty haze
of diamond – deep commitment.

In Opal Fields he bought a gem
and found another, more perfect yet –
a haven for a wounded soul,
a caring warmth that crept in quietly,
healing him whole.

Like summer mists
the opals gleam,
a flaming foil to twinkling gems;
and the diamonds rare
are yet less so,
than the honest warmth of long ago.
In the opals, now, what glows for me
are soul and care in synchrony –
the kindness fair that seems to be
forever Opal Fields.

In Opal Fields
he bought a gem but found,
far sweeter yet,
the warmth of friends.

Like a jute sack

Like a jute sack,
my face
is a mask of melancholy,
drooping,
sagging,
serviceable,
recycled for another year.

I feel like an old bag
past its prime;
piteous yet pleading,
daunted but still flaunting
my strong composition,
that inner will
that refuses to be thrown away.

I tell myself
I am not glass to shatter,
nor artificial,
pasting
plastic-smiles
on cosmetic-cheeks.
I am world-weary,
a little tired, perhaps,
but I have integrity.
Like a jute sack,
I am worn,
but still have my uses.
My melancholy
dissipates to quiet conviction.

This vast valley of sound

Whence come those silent whispers,
creeping into my soul, colouring my thoughts,
blinkering my mind?
I was quiescent, calm, almost happy
until they kicked the portals of my world and entered,
unbidden.

Now they are a voiceless noise drumming at my
conscience,
thrumming ceaselessly on my heartstrings.
In silence I hear those bitter tremors, discordant and
jarring,
resonant, alarming, ringing, raining shuddering bursts
of
merciless screams on my otherwise harmonious self.

Where do they come from,
those flitting fancies, those long shadows that belong
nowhere near the doorsteps of my heart?
How dare they kick the portals of my soul
and enter, unbidden?
Half formed and half whole, they creep
To the cold corners of consciousness,
taking hidden space. They take quarter where none is
given
and place where none is granted.

And in those spaces, they create an orchestra of
troubles,
a symphony of soundless hell that strikes
timpani and bells, clatter and dells of lonely discord.

It is impossible to quiet the noise of internal
perspective,
to ignore the sudden clamour of passing thoughts,
the beating of guilt on drums,
the low hum, the endless strum of conscience or
kindness,
that comes unbidden, and interferes with
quiescence and calm.

I have come to think of this noise,
this vast valley of sound as my freedom and my curse.
Without it I would have peace, but it would be the
peace of the blind
and the stillness of the morally deaf.

I would rather hear the shrieks and the clatter
and the thundering pulse of my veins
than turn my back on who I am.

Paradise

What is paradise?
There are many versions of this dream.

Let's examine
what the premise means.

Paradise
is a stasis of time,
a lengthening of years;
eternal youth,
perpetual truth
in a world
devoid of tears.

But happiness
is always at another's expense.

Unless one sits on a fence,
there will be the victor and the defeated;

the cause you take up
and the one you ignore.
And ignored, will it not be worse than ever before?

And will not winning
be empty defeat
unless you triumph
and actually beat
some other poor person,
who also had dreams,
now broken and lost,
and ripped at the seams?

You may say you want all to do well.
You may believe, of course,
the lies you tell.
But isn't it true you want to do better?
You must be that braver or richer go-getter?

If all got top marks,
there'd hardly be a point, which means all tests are
sadly out of joint
in a paradise dispensing (and it must, we agree)
universal delight to all that we see.

So paradise, then, is not what we thought;
there must be battles lost in each war fought.

There must be hopes that are harnessed
where others are flung.
There must be melodies mute
while some are still sung.

It must be a place of contrasts.
There must be exhaustion to savour leisure,
dross for every silken treasure;
experience to balance youth,
lies for every spoken truth.

In short, if I had a wish for paradise,
a simple dream,
it would not be
no thoughts that are cruel,
no thoughts that are mean.
It would not be
all pure and all kind and all clean.

It would be more, let the contrast be fair.
Let people who strive
be the ones to compare
their victories with those
in the throes of defeat;
so the people who lose,
are the people who cheat.

Let no child start
without hope or a chance,
born to despair with no scope to advance.

If the playing field starts even,
then paradise is won.

So it's not light above,
but right below,
in fabrics that are
fairly,
squarely,
silk-soft
spun.

I'd rather bear a fractured heart

If I was bathed in happiness, perfect in its glow,
I'd see the plight of others – but wouldn't stop to know.

And herein lies the puzzle, herein lies the key.
Perfection is not perfect if it uplifts only me.

How can I bathe in happiness,
fears and fancies fled,
when the blood of a child soldier
drenches deep and dark stained red?

How can I smile,
my heart so light and free,
when half a world away,
a generation's taught to flee?

What is comfort,
as there are women whipped for thought?
What my pride and careless ease,
as slaves are sold and bought?

If stop I did,
my happiness, too,
would dim;
for empathy, both gift and curse,
is so oft cold and grim.

Yet, if I were happy,
and looked not,
saw not,
my heart could not be whole,
the trio of my spirit,
the solace of my soul –
all that would be lost to me,

oh, high, so high a price!
I cannot yearn for happiness,
if its comfort is a vice.

So, it's not happiness I seek.

For while there is injustice,
while there is intolerance,
while there is cruelty –
my joy would just be bleak.

What do I hope for?

I hope for change, for outrage, and for caring.
I dare the world to pause with Valentine's day,
PlayStations, Olympic Games and all that fuss.

Stop a moment, look at us!
Where is our perspective, where our soul?
Can we be happy if our hearts are not whole?
Can our hearts not be fractured once we've begun?

I think not, I hope not.
I'd rather bear a fractured heart
than oh, an empty one.

Cogito ergo sum:
ode on intimations of dementia

I'll never grow old
or uselessly cold,
if my thoughts,
bright and soft-bold,
unfurl and unfold in a ream of bright gold
and are mine, mine to have and to hold.
So long as they shine
and occasionally gleam,
streaming bright for all I've meant and still mean,
I'll not fall into the trap of shadows.

I'll not live in half light –
I don't think I can.

If ideas are snatched from me,
break my bones and my heart
and mourn not;
for without my reflections
I am no more me
than you are.
The totally of my experience
moulds me,
love drives me,
thoughts mesh me.
My thoughts are the refrain in the chorus of my life.

When my mind is emptied of these,
what remains will not be I,
but a lingering shadow,
flushed from some lesser stream.

I'd rather be enveloped in the soft hush of darkness
than in the harsh light of dreamless days,
seamless in their sameness,
mad in their monotony,
and emptied of all meaning.

Descartes once said, "cogito ergo sum,"
"I think, therefore I am."
I am, because I think.
And if I cannot have that privilege,
oh let me…
let me softly sink.

Freedom lost:
A contemplation of child labour

If I close my eyes to conscience, I reason with delight,
I can have it all in gems and jeans –
it's cheap,
it's fun,
it's right.
But my thoughts are quite annoying, they never let me be,
they make me think, and once I've thought,
touched the trinkets – all I've bought,
added costs (and losts) in short,
all I've wished
and all I've brought –
it doesn't add up.

No, it doesn't.

For
oh, these things,
these trifles cheap, are born of sighs,
of labours bleak,
the leatherette
of lives so cheap,
of laughter lost, of sundered sleep.
How do we all, as nations fair,
condone this wanton loss of care?
Can we countenance inner selves,
while buying bounty strewn on shelves,
made en mass
by sadder masses,
made of sighs and soft allases?

Can we wreak, with will well-spent, a better kind of firmament?

Perhaps.
Possibly.
Bye and bye.
It behooves us all at least to try.

Child Labour Free Accreditation,
UNICEF,
Labour laws,
attitudes…
ours.
Bi-partisan and absolute.

Lest conscience count the callous cost
of pennies spared –
for freedom lost.

You, who are my friends

I snap my fingers at the world,
the sad and stupid unwise world
that, all knowing,
describes the gift of love
as cloying,
and ascribes the search of spirit tawdry.

I look up to the shrine of my soul
and behold a place
untrodden by your steps or mine,
a path of simple purity,
forged by courage,
created by conviction.

And, in giving,
there is such certain lifting of heart,
such utter parting with world-worn ways,
that I am free.
And free,
I dismiss the weary sentiments of the worthy.
I dismiss the idle sneers of ignorance.
Released,
I place my trust, instead, in the worthwhile
truth of friends.

You, who are my friends –
known and not yet met –
you, who are my arbours,
lift me from the dust of the dreary
and uplift my waking soul.

There is no end to a love that is limitless.
It spills from me to you,
from us to each other,
from day to night,
from right to light,
to further light,
unending in its brightness.

It is a dawn more timid than the sun,
but, once met, once won,
is time transcendent.
The sun, silent,
must each day set.
But love,
once dawned,
is unmatched yet.

Celestial Promise

Not for me the niceties!

Not for me the niceties!
Strip me of their ties.
Strip me down to starkest truth. –
It's there that solace lies.
Let me stride, not walk
across the dark precipice,
battered by winds and hounded by storms.
Let me hold your hand and tame it,
this bridge that life adorns.
Let my heart sing
– not silent whisper –
the thoughts that set me free.

Let my tongue taste our hope's desire
and ever after,
let me be.
For you, my friend,
you laugh at the wind as you walk.
I cannot hear the harried howls
as I listen to you speak.
You talk in streaks of prismed-light,
each word unbrushed,
untouched by the pastelled-dust
of civility.

Instead,
your words are as bright as the breeze
that teases us,
warmer than the wind that seizes
our outstretched arms
and would have us freeze
on this craggy cliff-face.
They are lighter than the mists that embrace us,
truer than the air that we breathe.

I will listen,
striding on that teetering bridge of life,
bold because of you
and for you.
I will breathe life's joys and harness her whimsies.
I will be your light as you will be mine.
I will seize each moment and each moment twine
with yours.
Never will I leave.
Never,
on that daring precipice,
Will we e'er our hearts deceive.

My whispered wish

I'd like to think that when I'm long deceased,
and all that's left are embers of my life,
that something of the love I've fiercely felt
remains forever fast in hearts and minds.

I'd wish that something I once thought or said,
so brimmed with wisdom's well of fluid truth
that others flourished from my whims or words,
and breathed the substance of my strong beliefs.

If I can prove that kindness has import,
that living's not enough without some care,
that empathy's the key to burdened hearts,
unlocking's thus a fragile trust to earn.

Perhaps I'll prove that gold holds fast to thought,
that glitt'ring gems of good intent are mined
by digging, delving, touching, trying hard
to seize at joy, then seizing, share with all.

But jew'ls are flawed, and joy, like gold, alloyed.
There's always dross with every treasured day.
Illuminate the dreary, sad, opaque,
then cleave the light when clarity seems lost.

I whisper wishes to the wilds of winds
that my immortal hopes are sentient:
that when I'm gone, the feelings I have felt
remain to nurture-nourish those I've loved.

My air will be your aria

I sang a simple, whispered note, silent as a song,
not a song you'd sing with joy,
but quaver-rendered wrong.
My whispered note, it echoed soft, sad and flat-forlorn,
A muted tone 'pon passing breeze and sad,
how passing sad its form.

I sang again three single notes, then four or maybe more –
All, I fear, in minor key,
more mournful than before.

I sang my grief, my shattered dreams
on bitter, keening notes.
And the sounds, they hung on icy-winds
aloft, adrift, afloat.

But then the echoes,
around and abounding,
reeling, ringing, calling, sounding,
they bounced on the breeze,
and battered, returned,
transposed, transmuted,
half sung and half learned.

My halting notes, they lingered,
but their strident, bitter key
drifted softly into cadence
as the sweetness vanquished me.

For thoughts of you, my dearest one,
thoughts both kind and keen,
they shatter every darkness,
they sweeten every dream.

Celestial Promise

The rivers warble wet with song,
the grasses they sing your name,
in each mist there is a mention,
in each dawn – it's oh, the same.

I hear your echoes,
dearest one, in every rock and stone,
they're harmonies of purest peace
in symphonies full blown.

Now, no more
will I splinter sound like silence's thief,
or wet-shed tears at grabbing grief,
but rather, I will ever sing your song.

Oh, my air will be your aria,
my medley eons long.
I hear your echoes dearest one,
I am never far alone.

In melting into melody,
I've secret-sung you home.

Dell of dreams

You are right.

You and only you can touch my soul.
A soul, so unused to being touched,
so incredibly sensitive to any stroke,
no matter how careful,
how soft and how caring, that I cry.

My tears flow not from I,
my logical self, but from me,
that deep, irrational pool
that flows beneath my surface,
beneath I.

Beneath everything
I know and understand.

It is a wellspring of whispers,
a dell of dreams,
intangible as mists,
yet I cling to it,
for it is my very core.

Stubborn as self,
quiet as stealth,
it defies definition,
eluding empathy,
cloaking itself in the soft robes of the surreal.

It dares no man
or mind
to touch it.
Yet you do!

No wonder tears, taut with tension,
wet with silent
gratitude and stubborn grief, roll, unbidden,
'cross the boundaries of my soul's own self.

You touch my spirit
as you seek to drown the dark of depths
and seal my heart.

I hope,
oh, I hope
you can cut through my stubborn void
and heal
my hopes whole.

Dare

Sometimes a sweet day, soft and mellow and mild,
dulls the pain one feels within and the aching is defiled.

Ah, a conundrum – how, then, is this?
Does defiling of a negative
needs mark return of bliss?

No, for bliss is elusive,
it haunts not hearth but hell,
it whispers of some other earth
where "want" transforms to "well."

And "well" speaks of many things –
not love, not hearth, not plenty,
but all of these intertwined
'gainst syncopating empty.

And emptiness must needs be pain,
haunting and enduring –
there never is that other world, hallowed and alluring.

We grasp at it, we yearn, for sure – but always it
evades.

There is no earth but this our own –
and this a living haze.
A haze of torments all our own,
of living lost and wants undone,
of wishing we were still but young,
of wanting half the hurts but one,
and that one, that single, lonely one,
the trail of a heart undone.

For having loved, one wouldn't ever
forsake this truth – not once, not ever.
But being broken, shattered pride
must lead a life, must dark abide
the living hell, the dark divide,
the airless care this earth provides.

And only time can ever tell
if splintered heart can e'er be well.
And only kindness can be bliss
and only touch antithesis.

Touch me with your eyes,
finger through my soul,
that hearts embossed with care and cost,
just once might still find whole.
Touch me with your fingers fair,
trail them 'cross my spirit bare,
taste my tears, my weeping, share,
then take that leap and caring,
dare.
Dare, defiant dare,
lest my emptiness flood everywhere.

To die for

Spinning a web
of deceit
from dry leaves
and yesterday's lies,
I wait for a victim
and slowly drip poison
from my silken under-things.

I extend myself lazily,
catching the sun's glint
on my squat body.
At this angle, I am cracked and hairy.

No matter,
I can twist myself into the silken strands,
embedding myself in soft sheets
of invitation.

No-one notices ugliness
when it is cloaked thus,
I have discovered.

I twist my twine
with curious flicks of concentration.
Premeditated lust, not happenstance.
I jeté a slow, sensuous dance
to the centre of my universe, self consciously limber.

Another provocative stretch as I seal
the silk in perfect little circles,
all designed,
with stealthy precision,
to ensnare.

I watch:
two souls dangling.
Oh,
yesterday's catch.
They're breaking my web. So gauche.

I sigh,
already slightly bored.
Tedious,
all that slow suffering.
I regard my manicure with interest.
Black claws with vicious little edges.
Honestly,
to die for.

Phase IV
New Moon Darkness

Grief resolution, social conscience
and regeneration to light

I'll watch how wild the poppies grow

Ah Gallipoli!

Like rain,
my tears stain not just my face
but the blood of the endless bodies,
and that blood,
wet-streaked with grief,
pulses my constant refrain.

The slain lie deep in the drifts,
fly-blown, wind-wept, silent.
Some whole, some half-limbs,
some the merest fragments
of what might have been.

You sting me still,
your biting winds, your searing heat,
your trenches, dark and dank.
The bodies a-tumble like autumn leaves
drenched, drenched by the rains and rank.

Gallipoli!
I bleed for you still,
and my blood, deep and dark and wet,
is the blood of the far-off fallen,
pulsing dread I can't forget.

Let us grieve, for certain,
let us leave the stains of our tears
in the groves and long-dug graves.

Gallipoli! Our hearts still bleed
for the senseless, the needless
toll you've craved.

We gave brave men's hearts
and the keening of women,
all a-weeping,
and whilst they keened and while they cried,
heart-rich in red refrain,
a stumbling mass of the thirsty,
the killing, the frightened,
they answered your call, Gallipoli,
they answered your call and came.

Sing to me, the weepers,
the widows forged of thee.
Sing to me the quiet bereft, ye nation's odyssey.

More than a beach, splattered with long gone blood,
more than a battle, mapped on foreign soil,
more than a nation's memoir.

Teach us of freedom fought dearly,
of statehood so hard won,
forge reason from futility,
oh slain,
ye slain of Anzac's sons.

Then,
I'll watch how wild the poppies grow,
rich and bright and red. They grow free upon the banks,
as they shroud our endless dead.

Annette

She was the wellspring,
the fountain,
the unendable
tide.

She was the pivot
and the pivotal,
the clock whose hands
pointed ever
to the hour of homecoming;

whose chimes
chimed always of warmth,
of a generosity of spirit
that was matchless;
of a love
that was boundless,
endless,
resistless;
ungovernable both in its force and in its tenor.

Oh, to hear those chimes again!
To hear,
just once,
the cadent ticking,
heady, ready, simple, steady.
To be enveloped again
in the cog-springs of that heart.

There is no other tide like hers,
no other clock,
or charm or chime.

But listen closely
for the echoes,
for the gentle ticking of that heart-clock.

It beats yet.

It beats, Annette,
in the minds of those you've touched.

In countless hearts it beats,
and yes,
it beats in mine.

Give not, grant not

Fling dread
further than earth's rim,
further,
far past the brim
of our cascading world,
fathoms past
our ringing pleas
and dark demands
for vengeance.

Fear,
far flung,
clings with cloying
certitude to every fallen whim.
A bringer
of those phantoms of half-light
ringing in new,
grim spectres.

Give not, grant not,
feed not its fury,
but fling it far;
that its echo
resonates in the wilderness,
and no longer
rests with us.

Garland us,
oh people,
with flowers
from the fields.

Bathe us in light,
not shadows,
sing us the songs
yet unsaid
and speak not,
no none among you,
of fears unshed
nor
darkness dread.

In memoriam: September the eleventh

The branches break with the liturgy of lament;
and yet, there is more.
The tide has not turned, nor will it ever.
Step forward, one foot at a time,
that you may be counted in this
shattered outpouring of anguish.

Tread carefully,
lest your footprints are lost in the dust.
Languish, oh hearts, in the brave ash of what once was,
but is no more.

Yet it is in the very heart of darkness
that man finds his strength.
It is not bones that will crush him, but despair.
It is not ash and dust that choke him,
but outrage.

Grieve! Grieve all you people of the world,
all you makers and masters of humanity!
Grieve, for those you have lost,
for the lives, ever changed, that are left!

I weep, and my tears do not begin to fill the void
that has been left us.
I sigh, and my sighs
are not echoed loudly enough in the wind.

Do not step bleakly, or blankly,
but boldly.
Walk, for those you have lost have loved you,
have leaned on you,
have learned and lived
and laughed with you.

Let it be their laughter
that rings in your ears,
their scents
that sweeten the sad tide
that rises like an ocean
from the furthest shores
of this curved, cusped world.
A crush of fears
that should break our very backs,
but won't.

Nothing will ever be the same.
In their name, for their sakes,
let us douse the flames
but keep the candles burning.

When shall we five meet again?

When shall we five meet again?
A simple, sad, yet sweet refrain.
Death is sweeping, leaves its stain
on those who pass and those remain.

I wonder, oft, if there is more,
beyond our furthest, far off shore.
Beyond the known, the furthest moon,
and if there is, is there room?
Is there shelter, is there light
to darken this, the dark of night?

I wonder, but getting no answer I weary.
For all I see and all I know,
carried shrill and echoed slow,
is the shallow, hollow,
resounding "no"
that bites into my soul.

If I believed in ever after,
the echoes might reverberate differently.
Perhaps the hollows of the hills would
bend and bounce, rend the echoes lightly, brightly,
whisp'ring of promises.

But I do not believe,
so clutching at the straw of false comfort
consoles not a whit.

We five shall not meet again,
on this or yet another plain.
We will die,
as others do,
first the one, and then a few.

First me perhaps, or maybe you,
but death will come, its sentence true.

There is only one way to fight it,
and that is now.
Now the living – bold somehow –
with our breath and with our souls,
with our aims and with our goals,
with our care, with our comfort, with our kindness,
let us tease and let's cajole,
let us laugh, but laugh with soul.

We are one,
a fam'ly whole,
perhaps our best, most perfect role.
In living now and loving true,
we kick at death and death shall rue,
for while it takes at cutting cost,
our living bond
shall ne'er be lost.

Elizabethan sonnet 1

Compare me not to some sweet summer's day

Answer to Shakespeare's Sonnet 18,
'Shall I compare thee to a Summer's day?'

Compare me not to some sweet summer's day,
nor alter winds with words sooth-soft for me,
I'm drenched and dragged in snow-drifts, come what may,
in thund'rous storms I flail, so let me be.

At times too pitch the gates of private Hell:
All known, I'm doomed to see and slow forget:
the brightest things, from woods to flowered dell,
entombed in mists of darkest, dense, regret.

Eternal summer faded with my youth,
when brightest sun fell shattered from the sky.
The world's all lies... all damnèd splintered truth,
thus languish ice, as seasons surely die.

So long as loy'lty's lost – and heart's alone,
so long shall freeze my heavy heart of stone.

Elizabethan sonnet 2

My master's teeth are nothing like the snow

In humorous contrast to Shakespeare's Sonnet 130,
'My mistress' eyes are nothing like the sun'

My master's teeth are nothing like the snow.
They reek, forsooth, with cavities untold.
If wits be quick, why then his thinking's slow:
if handsome's shy, why then my lord is bold.

My master sings a rough and roared duet,
great gusts of garlic never far from tongue.
The notes and pitch, alas, he'll oft forget –
but trust me true: no song he leaves unsung!

At night I try in vain to stop his snore,
close fast my eyes to his unsightly chest,
but though, at times, he tends to slightly bore,
his heart is sound, more goodly than the rest.

Despite complaint, I love with starry eyes:
with plainest truth: not garnished, silk-soft lies.

Mantra of the living dead

It's not the sense of moral authority,
'though ethical superiority
is a rare and unexpected gift.
And the more one comes to think on it,
the more, perhaps, it is about ethics;
about caring, sharing and never plundering more than
the planet has to give.
Why, after all, are we so needy,
so sincerely greedy that it becomes necessary
to force-feed ducks for their pate,
paralyze and immobilize chickens
in their billions,
pigs in their millions
and sheep?
Why ship sheep alive, so they may be fresh dead?
Sometimes I think we are crazed,
seriously muddled in our head,
last to voice the loud unsaid,
masters of the living dead.
Are we really so stupid that we can't see that stealing
is stealing,
same as if from me,
the looting of the honey bee?

A bee works the whole of its life for a teaspoon of
honey
and we rape its room,
smoke its hive with fuss and fume,
kill its queen,
divide its loom,
drive in droves to separate dooms.

Then,
lick a little,
spoon a spoon,
drizzle, spread,
spill or fume that we're out of jam or cheese or feta...
honey's sweet, but bacon's better.
We have become thoughtless and heartless,
uncaring for anything but ourselves and our needs.
The irony is it is not our needs
we are serving but our ignorant wants.
Like ants they crawl over our soul,
ripping asunder honest hunger
and blanketing simple need in a cloth
we are socialized to accept as right.
I call it the cloak of greed.
I call it excessive to want the liver of a chicken,
the tongue of an ox, the fat of a pig,
the leg of a lamb, the egg of a mother.
We have freedom of choice,
a choice to live better,
breathe leaner,
harvest health
and kindness cleaner.
We ingest death's own dice
and see it not as sin or vice.
We munch on bones and skin and fat
and close our eyes to the pain.
Not the pain of the butcher's knife,
not the throat slitting,
the blood-letting,
the refrigeration of the dead,
but the pain of being.

I once saw the gaze of a sheep on a sheep truck.
It looked at me directly
and bore into my soul.

I was revolted by the smell of faeces and urine
and averted my eyes.
I told myself it was a creature born to this doom,
but my heart never did believe my lies.
I once saw a chicken bound and inverted,
its legs chopped off before its head.
It was alive –
another of our living dead.

We choose to do this,
it doesn't just happen.
There is no mitigation for us,
as we grow fat, diabetic, sick and bloated.
No mitigation for the sullying of our seas
and the salting of flesh,
for the cries of calves,
for the kiss of death
that lingers on breeze-blown grass.
They are curse and promise,
what is past is not past and our folly and fears
shall make it last long, unless we find a better way.

And is it so bad
to eat less and savour more,
from vine to tree to forest floor?
We need less than we think
and the earth is bountiful and our imagination rich.
Rich from the soil,
more recipes abound,
more possibilities open up
than ever I have found
at the collective hunting grounds
of the obese.
Let us leave
the mantra of the living dead
and choose the song of life instead.

Greek mythology cycle: Songs of the siren[i]

1. The seeking songs of Strimadees:
a ballad of death

A secret smile is solace
when the nights grow chill and long,
when the candles gut
to waxen heat,
when night-sound's but a song.
The song of the Siren Strimadees, her whispers silk-
soft long,
her call allure
and luring…but
cadence trust – trussed wrong.

Ah, many a man has fallen, so many a man has wept,
at the haunting notes half-human,
in languish long regret.
They've listened long to siren's song,
half hope; half truth; half curse;
are bound,
rebound
and dark confound
by spells they can't reverse.
In awe they hear her, Strimadees,
so wild upon the waves…
the rhythms of her reason, her quatrain-quavered
staves.

For Strimadees,
half-hope, half curse,
half silken tongue in spangled verse,
half sensual touch,
not e'er averse,
to ling'ring thoughts that wanton nurse,

the strum of hope, made mad, made worse,
by her golden, gated,
universe.

"Sing to me, oh Strimadees,
of all your love, your care,
your joys, your heart, your whispered wish,
and let me love you fair."
"I will forsooth, in words and truth,
but love, like life, expands,
the universe grows, and ne'er-naught slows,
its exponential strands.
My love for you, sooth-sung so true,
is strong and unabashed,
but like the sea,
now swells so free, 'cross other hearts salt-washed.

"Many are the mariners
my heart has bound to me, awash with wary
wistfulness,
and not a one now free.
For a siren's love is not contained,
it has no end or lid,
it flows and flows from dusk to dawn – it always has
and did.
And so my dearest mariner,
I'll lead you to your doom,
spell-drenched, my songs shall guide you
as hopes of me
entomb.

"I love and hate
and bind and bond,
I'm the siren Strimadees.

I toss and tease
from world's beyond
on whim, on wind,
on salt-swift breeze.
So let me drown you mariner,
in the sweetest of caress,
like other men have fallen,
yet deemed their doom
success.

"Other men have loved me,
other men have sighed,
and dying,
heard my siren's call,
sultry soft and wanton-all,
the secret song, the madrigal,
the bliss-bled notes,
tormented, all,
yet honey-drenched in haloed thrall,
those minds, those hearts, those mariners all.

"Thus on willful nights when the waves accost,
when an eerie hum, all notes embossed,
when harmonic scales in chords now lost,
are sung by me, in seas well tossed,
then heed your heart oh sailor,
heed your heart and soul,
for my touch is light, my lure alight,
and the dark shall weave us whole.
Oh seekers, seekers,
come to me; over sails and over seas,
hark the calls, in chords and keys,
the seeking songs of Strimadees."

2. The betrayal of Persephone

When the wail of wind
and salt-rushed sea
binds man to mast in agony,
when rains rush wild and all the light
is demon-dark in mist-bled night,
then comes to man, 'bove haloed height,
the sirens' isles,
a strange-sweet sight.

Cast-off
upon yon craggy rocks,
alone, adrift at sea,
the Sirens sing their mournful songs,
and their souls sing out to me.

"But why?" I ask,
"but why, oh yes, oh why?
do maids so shy, like gods on high,
condemn free men to die?"

And the sirens sang their answers when the mists were
white and curled,
they lured me close to listen
as they sang about my world.

"Once, upon a far off time
when the meadows were but green,
when the fruits of all our harvests
were buds still yet unseen,
when we nymphs were dear,
the skies still clear,
And Demeter in her sleep,
the underworld awakened
and darkened all she'd reaped.

Celestial Promise

Ah,
but for a lingering moment,
(a moment long and sweet)
the cruelest glance of Hades
was the gaze of God made meek.
For the daughter of Demeter,
with a smile that lit the sun,
was the breath of purest heaven
that left Hell
quite heart-undone.

"But a heart
in the heart of Hades.
beats wanton-dark with lust,
and the pulse of passion's pleasure
becomes the trampled pain of trust.

"And we?
We the smiling maidens,
bedazzled by his charm,
puppet-danced to shadows,
and quelled our keen alarm.
We danced the dance of sirens,
so slow, so subtle sweet,
but the night adrift with secrets
glowed doors beneath our feet.

"Thus it was Persephone,
fair maiden-nymph of glades,
was dragged in damnèdst weeping
to the living hell of Hades.

"And we,
her falt'ring maidens,
fell
weeping to our knees:

begged mercy for high
failure,
in shamed
and rasping pleas.

"And in the dark, Persephone,
in wells and wells so deep,
could hear no call or kindness,
could life
ne'er feel nor keep.

"Winter freezes earth,
the rain shall ne'er once cease.
There buds no growth nor blossom,
nor tiny sprouting peace.

"Demeter bargains, Zeus wavers,
but time –
time is now cut short –
the bargains turn to pleading,
the pleading so hard fought

"Persephone starves, in darkest dream,
tastes fruited seeds, all sight unseen;
and tasting,
feels,
feels it keen,
her crowning
as the dark-wed queen.

"And we, her maids, in hell above,
abandoned, loathed, and lost to love
were granted wings
to search her path,
searched every stone 'pon every hearth
But falt'ring, failed, incurred the wrath

of every god
her kindness passed.

"So,
We were bound by blood and cast to sea,
cast to sing, and sing so free
the sirens' songs, in symphony,
as harlots high,
in harmony.

"Profound, profound and all around,
the echoes clear across the sound,
the answers dark, the damage keen,
we're bondage-bound to
the dark-world queen.

"Mariner, mariner,
we now confess,
that songs once sweet
like maidens' breath,
are sullied notes; the dark caress
of Hades' call,
the calls to death!"

3. The sirens to the mariner[ii]

Whom shall we honour?
Whom shall we spare?

Him who entangles hope in bright snares,
to logic-bind our nightly mares.

Him,
so wise so wise before our eyes,
dissecting truth
from tale-dipped lies,
that truths well shaded,
once so hidden,
reveal our hearts,
so long forbidden.

Yes,
we'll spare
him who thinks or cares,
who trysts with truth
and caring, dares;

So wise so wise before our eyes,
dissecting truth
from tale-dipped lies,
that truths well shaded,
once so hidden,
reveal our hearts,
so long forbidden.

We'll spare
him who thinks or cares,
who trysts with truth
and caring, dares;
dares see who we
were born to be,
beyond these hags
'pon rock or sea,
free spirits trapped,
trapped are we,
by cursed fate, by damned decree,
in the wreakèd wrath
of deities.

And you will hear,
we now aver,
we're maidens fair who once did err,
once lived the life we'd fain prefer,
with innocence stripped, profane concur.

Pity us, oh sailor, pity us our soul;
compassion's truth might touch our youth,
and find us once heart-whole.

Then, sailor dear,
from us to you,
race the seas,
go sail anew,
stop your ears with wax or glue,
lest our sirens' will
betray us,
too.

4. Circe to the sirens[iii]

All power to the sirens three,
sisters, sisters unto me,
blood of gods
and of the sea,
daughter, I, to Hecate.
I watch the sirens' power grow,
their songs of grief overflow
in shifting scales from high to low,
their innocence ripped all long go.
I watch them weave, with their tongues,
the strands of lust, one by one,
temptations all, 'neath sea-soaked sun,
granted by the shaded one.
For Hades of the dark and deep,
the underworld their rocks shall reap,
the shipwrecked bones of all they seek,
the sirens three
of Scoplus' Leap.

But I am Circe wild and free,
the blood of Helios flows in me,
the God of sun and Hecate,
witch and wild and potent, see,
the potions I can gift to thee.
Come hither, mariners, hear my call,
sirens true are not at all
as silken soft or peaked or tall, as Circe's touch,
or wherewithal.
With potions, I am utmost power.
Come seek ye solace
through my bower,
where sweet caress turns teasing-sour
as seconds chime to wretched hour.

For on my isle of Aeaea,
high above the trees,
I gather herbs and mysteries
far greater than the seas.
More potent than the sirens' breath,
more callous than a shipwrecked death, more strange,
by far,
'neath Helios' star, the arts and spells I do attest.
From the dust of earth to butterfly,
transform I must, transform must I,
that man shall squirm and squeal and sigh
like muddied pigs in sullied sty.
And with my potions,
he who yearns for lust-filled days in spring-trilled
turns,
with sweetest temptings he shall learn to bark like dog,
or bray concerns.
And barking, baying, growing, curse
the love of Circe,
love made worse
by that far-off, fated
universe.

Betrayal, sirens, all the same,
from darkest hell to island tame,
wreak your wrath,
but sing my fame
For pigs *do* fly –
where I once came.

5. Regeneration

Ah Persephone…
Tunnels dark where bones do seek,
The faint-dread heart
of sailors meek,
Now Hades, hers,
but heart oblique,
as darkness quells
her hopes now bleak.

And the world above,
devoid of love,
is winter,
chill
and bland,
Demeter (hand upon her heart) wills land
to unsown sand.

Now leaves, in autumn weeping, drop tears from
seeping skies,
and the gods' clear wrath are reaping, in the deep
where Hades lies.
"Bring her back, yon maiden,
she never was your wife,
you stole from her
her youthful spring, and owe her now her life."

Lo! Hades sick of winter,
of freezing in the snow,
with grudging shrug a-creeping,
let the summer nymph just go.
Now Persephone, released from deep,
awake at last from dell-drugged sleep,
alone she pleads in voice so meek,
redemption for the Sirens bleak.

From fair to foul and foul to fair,
brighten now the summer air,
fill the glades in symphony,
trill sweet songs in synchrony,
peal bright bells, in hills and dells
and bathe in light
Persephone.

Fear: a palindrome[iv]

Alone.
Fear frightens Dusk,
forever
percolating dread.

Fancies flitter fleetingly.
Unheard, unanswered thoughts
are invasive intrinsically.

Steadily rising hackles:
rampant turmoil within.

Black, nightmare tremors whispering
deep, obscure dreams.
Subtly painting anxiety dark,
extrapolating
dark anxiety: painting subtly.
Dreams: obscure, deep,
whispering tremors: nightmare black.

Within, turmoil: rampant
hackles rising steadily.

Intrinsically invasive are
Thoughts; unanswered, unheard.
Fleetingly flitter, fancies,
dread percolating
forever.

Dusk frightens fear:
alone.

Joy: a palindrome[v]

Joy
illuminates hope,
always influencing and
brightening bold thoughts.
Enchantment waltzing with laughing light,
feelings sweetening conceptions,
thus inspirations impart
smiling sparkles of incandescence.
Forever glittering,
radiant happiness

echoes

happiness radiant,
glittering forever:
incandescence of sparkles, smiling,
impart inspirations thus.
Conceptions sweetening feelings,
light laughing with waltzing enchantment,
thoughts, bold, brightening
and influencing – always.
Hope illuminates
Joy.

I am the moon

Dark with terror,
I'm engulfed in dread.
I'm sober, somber and absolute.
My thoughts are wickedly black.
I soak in the silence, cocooning myself in bleakness.

Gradually, I become aware of light.
There is a faint wisp of it streaming behind me,
and though I cling to the darkness,
I am mindful that I can no longer ignore its touch.

Now, I'm suspended on a moonbeam,
adrift in a silk-soft yearning
that thrums with a whisper of promise.
Quietly, hardly noticing, I am caressed into my second self.

I am the moon, casting darkness into wisps of light,
growing ever more steady
with each of my risings.

I still feel my pain, but it is mitigated by hope, and the hope becomes
fuller, more bountiful, until I am smiling.
I am the smiling moon.
My beauty is boundless, bolder than my fears.

I turn my face to the sun and there are now no tears,
only the fullness of joy and generosity of spirit that
centres me whole.

I am bathed in light, impelled to reflect its glory.
I turn my face on the world and in this fullness, my
brilliance brings wonder.

Moonstruck,
I am heady with my glow, steady in the fullness of fulfillment.

I touch the tides and caress the earth in luminescence.
I am, for a single, perfect instant, all that there is to be.

To know such deep perfection, to be bathed in its light,
to radiate its warmth, is ultimate ecstasy.

But with wholeness comes
Responsibility, with responsibility, commitment.

I am touched, ever so slightly, by shadows. Ah, and with these graver thoughts,
still smiling, I am plummeted into my final phase.

I have felt the darkness of despair and found my zenith.
I have waxed, and now I wane.

With serenity, I find the solace of the skies.

I dip, slightly, to temper the darkness of the coming phase.
My reward, as I fade, is starlight.

My brightness had obliterated its beauty. I am humbled.
As the heavens twinkle, I find myself subsiding.

I've lost my heady joy, but I'm content.
The new moon, dark in its solitude,
will need me.
I'll be there.

Epilogue

Now phases of the moon,
played out in poetry,
grow once more
and orbit our world
in the pearly glow
of comfort,
kindness
and content.

Wear the mantle of our sun
and kiss our skies.
Your phases,
like ours,
are sometimes dark,
yet always you recover.
We'll watch your gleam
stream
from glimmer to smile,
from glow to radiance,
and in the cadence of gentle night
your fullness
will filter 'cross our earth,
crisp in clarity.

Our moon,
prism of promise bright,
passing on,
so-soft passing;
the sun's bright gift
of light.

Advance Response

I first encountered Hayley Ann Solomon as she was working on her novel *Wishbinder*, and as I became invested in the intriguing characters and engaging plot of this unique fantasy tale that was simultaneously fanciful and believable, I discovered very quickly that this author had a remarkable talent for creating worlds.

After reading through the poems of this collection, *Celestial Promise*, I see that my first impression was a valid one, for in these poems Ms. Solomon has recreated the world through her eyes and shared it with those fortunate enough to find this volume of her work.

Ms. Solomon takes the reader on a safari through several manifestations of the human condition. As with any safari, readers will be rubbernecking as this phrase and that catches their attention when they turn through the pages. Remember to keep all arms and legs inside the vehicle, and feel free to allow the specimens here on display to free the memories and feed the imagination. It will be an enjoyable ride.

Such expeditions can often include a frighteningly high probability of getting lost, but the way here is well lit as readers will be traveling by metaphorical moonlight along a lunar calendar which provides meticulous order to this meaningful journey. And of course, what better way to explore the human experience than with an excellent tour guide who creates new worlds in her spare time?

Randal A. Burd, Jr., M.Ed.
July 2, 2017

Advance Response

Celestial Promise provides us with a promenade through an adult's garden of verse: delighting in familiar, classical forms presided over by the lunar lens of a watchful moon. The poet is both romantic and scholar: inviting us to reflect on themes of transience and the cyclical nature of life: urging us to acknowledge the dark while reaching for the light.

Classical allusions and a strong mythical background provide pleasing, playful inversions: Ms Solomon has a solid grasp of form and uses its structures to roam freely and let her ideas sing.

Christopher Marlowe's shepherd receives a reply from his beloved nymph, one less cynical than Sir Walter Raleigh's rebuffal; the Sirens speak rather than sing to the mariners they intend to entrap; but the poet acknowledges love in its earthier, less rosy-tinted forms too: notably in the sonnet styled after Shakespeare: 'My Master's Teeth Are Nothing Like The Snow'.

Fear, joy, darkness, regeneration: Solomon's background in romance novels is reflected in the profound joy in all the forms of love that provide a wellspring for the poems in this structured, yet playful collection which finishes with the poet becoming the moon: content in all of its phases from gloom to luminescence.

Viki Holmes, author of *miss moon's class* (Chameleon Press, 2008), *Girls' Adventure Stories of Long Ago* (Chameleon Press, 2017) and co-editor of *Not A Muse* (Haven, 2009)

About the Author

Hayley Ann Solomon double-majored in English and Psychology (UCT); later graduating with an Honours Baccalaureus Bibliothecologiae (UNISA); followed by a Master of Arts degree in Library and Information Science (University of Victoria, Wellington). She has had many fiction novels published internationally, the majority under the *Zebra Regency Romance* label, New York.

She maintains a strong interest in poetic and literary genres, and her work has appeared in several short story anthologies, the most notable being the *Momaya Press International Annual Short Story Reviews* (2013 and 2015) and *Horizons 2: Winning Stories from Page and Blackmore National Short Story Competitions (2015)*.

Career highlights include the following: the choice of her novel, *Raven's Ransom* (2002), as "Top Pick" by the *Romantic Times*, her three times selection as Honoree for *The Binnacle*, University of Maine at Machias (2013-2014), being shortlisted for the Writers' Village International Short Fiction Award (2014); her selection by *Compose Literary Journal* for 'The Grasses are weeping' (2014;) and being placed first for 'The Chosen One' (New Zealand Society of Authors, Central Districts Competition 2015). She was also a finalist in the New Zealand Heritage Non Fiction Essay Award 2015.

In 2016, she achieved Fanstory All time Best Award for her Awdl Gynt cycle poem 'I hardly have the means or heart'. Her ecological poem 'Once green, now gone and grown no more' won a place in *Mingled Voices: The Proverse Poetry Prize Anthology 2016*.

Ms Solomon says poetry is a passion: she values the rich blend of cadence and cognition that makes poetry uniquely succinct, substantive and beautiful.

Her family's interests represent the cycle of life itself. She represents literature, her surgeon husband healing, her three sons the futures in science, law and computer engineering respectively. She lives amid olive groves and vineyards in Blenheim, New Zealand. She's a bel canto soprano with vibrant pink hair and a strong belief in kindness.

NOTES

[i] In Greek mythology, the sirens lured sailors to their death with their songs.

[ii] The sirens lured sailors to their deaths with song. Some say they were doomed by the betrayal of Persephone. Odysseus's crew stopped their ears with wax to save themselves from the fatal melodies. With exceptional foresight, Odysseus omitted the wax, but had himself lashed to the mast, immobilized by rope. He alone, therefore, heard – yet survived – the tormenting sweetness of siren song.

[iii] In Greek mythology, Circe was a powerful enchantress capable of turning men to swine. She appears in Homer's *Odyssey* along with the sirens – alluring creatures who entranced mariners with the ethereal promise of their songs, dooming them to death.

This ballad weaves classical mythology with my own interpretive mythology, a blend, if you will, of classical fiction with whimisical fiction – canon retelling, and the pure product of my imagination. While sirens feature in the history of Odysseus, specific named sirens do not. The character Strimadees is therefore my creation. The geography of Scoplus' Leap is also my own. I chose this name because "Leap" suggests a high, dangerous precipice with the allure of death. Scoplus has a Greek ring to it, suggestive of "scopus", which is a Latinisation of the Greek word for "watcher". The sirens were watchers, waiting for unwary mariners, so this seems apt. Further, there is a ridge of mountains east of ancient Jerusalem called Mt. Scopus – the name, therefore, is redolent of antiquity.

[iv] This poem and the next are palindromes, from dark to light. Palindrome poems are challenging sequences that read the same backwards or forwards, up and down, from left to right and right to left with minor adjustments for punctuation. The themes of fear and joy are chosen to echo the celestial cycle of darkness and regeneration.

[v] Another palindrome. Please see note iv, above.

ABOUT PROVERSE HONG KONG

Proverse Hong Kong is based in Hong Kong with expanding long-term regional and international connections.

Proverse has published novels, novellas, short-story collections, fictionalized autobiography, non-fiction (including autobiography, biography, Hong Kong educational and legal history, memoirs, travel narratives, sport), poetry and single-author poetry collections, academic and supplementary educational books, as well as children's and teens / young adult books. Other interests include diaries, and academic works in the humanities, social sciences, cultural studies, linguistics and education.

Some Proverse books have accompanying audio texts. Some are translated into Chinese.

Proverse welcomes authors who have a story to tell, wisdom, perceptions or information to convey, a person they want to memorialize, a neglect they want to remedy, a record they want to correct, a strong interest that they want to share, skills they want to teach, and who consciously seek to make a contribution to society in an informative, interesting and well-written way. Proverse works with texts by non-native-speaker writers of English as well as by native English-speaking writers.

The name, "Proverse", combines the words "prose" and "verse" and is pronounced accordingly.

THE INTERNATIONAL PROVERSE POETRY PRIZE
(SINGLE POEMS)

An annual international poetry prize (for single poems) was established in 2016. The international Proverse Poetry Prize (single poems) is open to all who are at least eighteen years old whatever their residence, nationality or citizenship.

Single poems, submitted in English, are invited on (a) <u>any subject or theme, chosen by the writer</u> OR (b) <u>on a subject or theme selected by the organizers each year</u>.

Poems may be in any form, style or genre. Each poem should be no more than 30 lines.

Entries should previously be unpublished in any way (except in the case of unpublished translations into English of the entrant's own work already published in another language, providing the entrant holds the copyright).

In 2016 and 2017, cash prizes were offered as follows:
1st prize; USD100.00; 2nd prize: USD45.00;
3rd prizes (up to four winners): USD20.00.

KEY DATES FOR THE PROVERSE POETRY PRIZE IN 2018 ONWARDS
(subject to confirmation and/or change)

Receipt of entered work, entry forms and entry fees	7 May to 30 June of the year of entry
Announcement of Winners	Before April of the year following the year of entry
Cash Awards Made	At the same time as publication of the winning poems (whether in the Proverse newsletter or website, or in an anthology)
Publication of an anthology of winning and other selected entries	Contingent on the quality of entries in any year

The above information is for guidance only.
More information, updated from time to time, is available from the Proverse website: proversepublishing.com

Celestial Promise

FIND OUT MORE ABOUT OUR AUTHORS, BOOKS, EVENTS AND LITERARY PRIZES

Visit our website: http://www.proversepublishing.com

Visit our distributor's website: <www.chineseupress.com>

Follow us on Twitter
Follow news and conversation: twitter.com/Proversebooks>
OR
Copy and paste the following to your browser window and follow the instructions: https://twitter.com/#!/ProverseBooks

"Like" us on www.facebook.com/ProversePress

Request our free E-Newsletter
Send your request to info@proversepublishing.com.

Availability
Most titles are available in Hong Kong and world-wide from our Hong Kong based Distributor, The Chinese University of Hong Kong Press, The Chinese University of Hong Kong, Shatin, NT, Hong Kong SAR, China.
Email: cup-bus@cuhk.edu.hk
Website: <www.chineseupress.com>.

All titles are available from Proverse Hong Kong,
http://www.proversepublishing.com
and the Proverse Hong Kong UK-based Distributor.

Stock-holding retailers
Hong Kong (Growhouse, Bookazine)
Singapore (Select Books),
Canada (Elizabeth Campbell Books),
Andorra (Llibreria La Puça, La Llibreria).

Orders from bookshops in the UK and elsewhere.

Ebooks
Many of our titles are available also as Ebooks.

www.ingramcontent.com/pod-product-compliance
Lightning Source LLC
Chambersburg PA
CBHW051129160426
43195CB00014B/2404